WATCHFIENDS & RACK SCREAMS

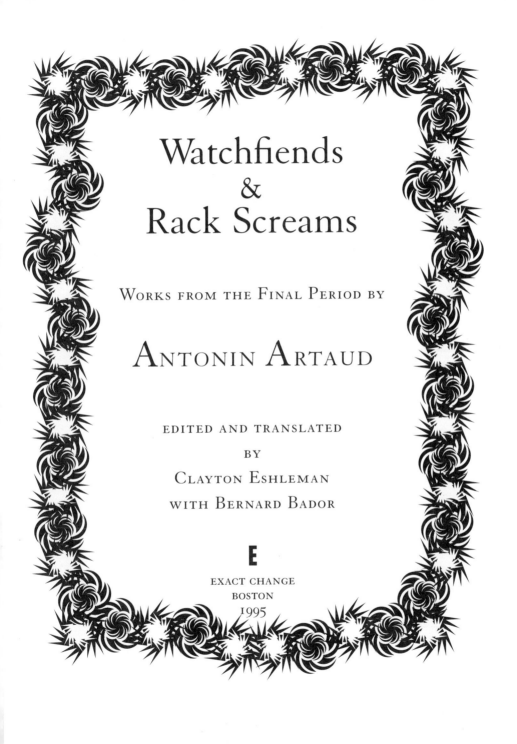

Watchfiends
&
Rack Screams

WORKS FROM THE FINAL PERIOD BY

ANTONIN ARTAUD

EDITED AND TRANSLATED

BY

CLAYTON ESHLEMAN

WITH BERNARD BADOR

E

EXACT CHANGE
BOSTON
1995

©1995 Exact Change

Originally published in French in volumes XI, XII, XIII, XIV*,
and XIV** of the *Oeuvres Complètes d'Antonin Artaud,*
©1974, 1978 Éditions Gallimard

All Rights Reserved
ISBN 1-878972-18-9

Ouvrage publié avec le soutien du Ministère Français de la Culture.
Grateful acknowledgement is made to the French Ministry of Culture
for financial assistance in the preparation of this translation.

Some of these translations first appeared in the following magazines:
Compost, Disturbed Guillotine, Grand Street, and *Sulfur.*

Cover paintings and endpapers by Nancy Spero.
Front cover: detail from *Codex Artaud XXIII,* 1972
Back cover: detail from *Codex Artaud XXIV,* 1972
Front endpaper: detail from *Codex Artaud V,* 1971
Back endpaper: detail from *Codex Artaud XXXII,* 1972
Artwork photographed by David Reynolds.

Exact Change books are edited by Damon Krukowski and
designed by Naomi Yang.

Contents

THE TRANSLATORS *dedicate this translation of Antonin Artaud's writings to the greatest of the "daughters of [his] heart," Paule Thévenin. From 1946 until her death in 1993, she dedicated her life to deciphering thousands of pages of Artaud's handwritten texts and letters, and anonymously editing thirty volumes — Artaud's Complete Works — for Gallimard.*

INTRODUCTION

BY CLAYTON ESHLEMAN

ANTONIN ARTAUD is one of the greatest examples in art of the imaginative retrieval of a life that was beyond repair. What he ultimately accomplished should bear a torch through the dark nights of all our souls. Given the new perspectives on his writing and drawing that he created in what may now be considered his second major period — from his regeneration in the Rodez asylum in 1945 to his death outside of Paris in 1948 — it seems especially pertinent to introduce a new translation of key works from this period with an essay that attempts to compactly yet fully detail the way his life and work intertwine and reverberate.

*

Antoine Marie Joseph Artaud, called Antonin (or "little Antoine," to distinguish him from his father), was born on September 4, 1896, in Marseilles, France. His father, a ship chandler, and mother, a Levantine Greek who married her cousin, had nine children, only three of whom survived. Such an excessive mortality rate may have been in part due to congenital problems which also played a role in Artaud's successive illnesses.

At four years old, he suffered terrible head pains from the onset of meningitis, one side effect of which led him to see double. In desperation (there was then no cure for acute meningitis), his father found and used upon the child a machine which produced static electricity, transmitted by wires attached to the person's head (prefiguring the electroshock treatments Artaud would receive in the Rodez asylum many years later). Whatever the alleged home cure's worth, he recovered, although he remained nervous and irritable throughout his youth. Between the ages of six and eight, he stuttered and experienced contractions of his facial nerves and tongue. "All this," he wrote in 1932, was "complicated by corresponding psychic troubles which did not appear *dramatically* until about the age of nineteen."[1]

Antonin was also deeply affected by the death of his seven-month-old sister, Germaine, when he was nine. Because the baby would not obey the commands of her nanny to stop crawling away from her, the nanny slammed Germaine down on her lap with such force that she perforated the baby's intestine, causing an internal hemorrhage from which she died the following day. Germaine haunted Artaud to the extent that much later he would induct her into his set of "daughters of the heart, to be born." Such "daughters," based on family members and friends, represented a repudiation of his own birth and a seeing of himself as the sole progenitor of a new family "tree."

In 1914, right before graduating from high school, Artaud had a nervous breakdown, destroyed his earlier poems, and gave away his library to friends. Extremely agitated, he prayed constantly and determined to become a priest (a religious crisis that would manifest itself again, with greater force, at Rodez). At this point, the family arranged various rest cures that, with the exception of a few breaks (one in which Artaud was briefly inducted into the army), continued for the next five years (again suggesting another early life/later life parallel: during the first World War, Artaud spent most of his time in clinics and thermal spas; for all of the second World War, he was incarcerated in five asylums).

In the year after his 1914 breakdown, Artaud later claimed he had been stabbed in the back by a pimp while walking down the street. The alleged assassin told him, he recounted, that it was not *he* who had perpetrated the attack; rather, at that moment, he had been possessed. In setting forth the first of some alleged half-dozen attacks on his life, Artaud was beginning the elaboration of a systematic "attack syndrome," composed of fact and probably fiction, in which evil forces were to ceaselessly obstruct his attempts to fulfill his destiny.

During 1917, suffering acute head pains and stormy, incomprehensible moods, Artaud, reading Baudelaire, Rimbaud, and especially Poe, was moved from clinic to clinic, at considerable expense to the family. He ended up, at the end of 1917, in a Swiss clinic, near Neuchatel, under the care of Dr. Dardel, who besides encouraging him to draw and write, also prescribed opium, setting up his lifelong addiction to drugs (and again prefiguring a later parallel: his ambivalent relationship at Rodez with Dr. Ferdière, who also encouraged him to translate and draw, during which he subjected him to electroshock treatments).

After two years in the Swiss clinic, Dr. Dardel proposed that Artaud strike out on his own and go to Paris. It was arranged for him to move in with Dr. and Mme. Toulouse, while the former was coincidentally engaged in a study on artistic genius. While Artaud had yet to begin his career as an actor, his theatrical bent is implicit in a photo from 1920, taken shortly before his departure for Paris. One sees a thin, sharp-featured, flowing-haired young man in coat and tie, head thrown back, eyes closed, wrists crossed over his breast, his long-fingered large hands clenched into fists. The figure seems at once laid out vertically, dead or asleep, and twisted in a paroxysm of inner torment.

*

Artaud's first set of years in Paris (1920-1936) were the most frenetic of his life. In order to fulfill his desire to become a film actor, he began taking roles in stage theater to obtain experience. While he achieved some memorable success as a film actor — notably as Marat in Abel Gance's "Napoleon" (1925) and as the monk Massieu in Carl Dreyer's "La passion de Jeanne d'Arc" (1927) — he discovered that he had no interest in commercial film making. However, he continued to act in films up through 1935, out of financial need, ultimately appearing in twenty films. Artaud's father died in 1924 (which ended family monetary support) and his mother moved to Paris to be closer to her children. From the mid-1920s on, Artaud was chronically broke (though capable of maintaining what had become a laudanum addiction), and he often moved in with his mother when he could not pay his rent. The combination of poverty and addiction relentlessly undermined his life and work during these years. His theater projects necessitated funding in order to be realized, and addiction destroyed his relationship with the actress Génica Athanasiou, with whom he had his only sustained love affair. In 1933, attempting to confront his addiction, he wrote:

> If I stop taking drugs, that means death. I mean that only death
> can cure me of the infernal palliative of drugs, from which only
> a precisely calculated absence, not too long in duration, allows
> me to be what I am. . . I can do nothing with opium, which is
> certainly the most abominable deception, the most fearsome

4

invention of the void which has ever impregnated human sensi-
bilities. But at any given moment, I can do nothing without this
culture of the void inside me.[2]

This "culture of the void" became an increasingly integral part of
Artaud's personality. Almost immediately after publication of his first
book — *Celestial Backgammon* (1923), an unimpressive collection of
stilted, quasi-surreal lyrics — he began to engage the editor of the pres-
tigious literary magazine, *La Nouvelle Revue Française* (henceforth
NRF), Jacques Rivière, in a correspondence that when published the
following year would put him on the literary map. Rejecting the closed
lyric in favor of the fragment, and agonizing over his inability to think
(by which he meant: to realize his imaginative energy at large in writ-
ing), Artaud ascribed his scatteredness to "a collapse of the soul" that so
undermined his physical sense of himself as to make him feel nonexis-
tent. Artaud was saying, in effect, that he refused to settle in writing for
anything less than expressing what he most truly felt was happening to
him. He worried in his letters to Rivière that someone or something was
deliberately invading his thought process and robbing him of what he
was attempting to express. This "higher and evil will attacking the mass
of feeling" is the progenitor of Artaud's later elaboration of fiends and
doubles pillaging not only his thought but his bodily fluids.

Much of Artaud's Rivière correspondence would have fit right in
with his second and third books, *The Umbilicus of Limbo* and *Nerve-
Scales* (both 1925). Composed of fragments, a play, theater manifestoes,
denouncements of literature ("All writing is pigshit"), reworked letters,
and descriptions of paintings, these books are generally described as
prose poems. While such a description is superficially acceptable, it fails
to indicate the diversity of the literary genres involved which would, in

the 1940s, be braided into single pieces of writing: letters, for example, that at the same time were poems, chants, manifestoes, and essays. In these books of 1925, Artaud relentlessly complains of feeling paralyzed, abyssal, absurd; he is without works, a language or a mind that he can respect. He seems to refuse to bypass or attempt to transcend this negativity because he feels that within its turbulence is a power that if transformed will put him at one with himself:

> . . . Thinking means something more to me than not being completely dead. It means being in touch with oneself at every moment; it means not ceasing for a single moment to feel oneself in one's inmost being, in the unformulated mass of one's life, in the substance of one's reality; it means not feeling in oneself an enormous hole, a crucial absence; it means always feeling one's thought equal to one's thought, however inadequate the form one is able to give it.[3]

While Artaud's differences with official Surrealism are fundamental, his two year (1924-1926) involvement with it is understandable. The Surrealist contempt for bourgeois values, and their fascination with ritual, the subconscious, dreams and trances, excited the ambivalent poles in Artaud that despised society and affirmed the possibility of drawing upon what Gary Snyder has called "the Great Subculture," that rich vein of African, Eastern, and esoteric Western materials, some of which, via Surrealism, were making their way into the poetic consciousness of the 1920s.

Artaud briefly ran the Surrealist Research Center, which had previously been open for the public to come in and record their dreams (Artaud closed the Center to the public and unsuccessfully tried to use it for disciplined Surrealist research). He also contributed to the first two issues of the official Surrealist magazine, *La Révolution surréaliste,* and edited and wrote most of the third issue. At the same time he continued to act in commercial films, and with the former (expelled) Surrealist poet Roger Vitrac and the writer Robert Aron attempted to launch the Alfred Jarry Theater. Both of these activities brought him into conflict with the inflexible Surrealists, who despised commercial film making and disputed Artaud's association with Vitrac. The Surrealists — chiefly André Breton — also suspected that all theater was bourgeois and profit-oriented, and were on the verge of an alignment with the French Communist Party, an alignment which Artaud, who maintained all revolution must be physical (as opposed to political), could not abide. At the end of 1926, Artaud and Phillipe Soupault — Breton's former co-author of *The Magnetic Fields* — were officially expelled.

Susan Sontag articulates Artaud's temperamental differences with the Surrealists: "The Surrealist, he thought, was someone who 'despairs of attaining his own mind.' He meant himself, of course. Despair is entirely absent from the mainstream of Surrealist attitudes. The Surrealists heralded the benefits that would accrue from unlocking the gates of reason, and ignored the abominations. Artaud, as extravagantly heavy-hearted as the Surrealists were optimistic, could, at most, apprehensively concede legitimacy to the irrational. While the Surrealists proposed exquisite games with consciousness which no one could lose, Artaud was engaged in a mortal struggle to 'restore' himself. Breton sanctioned the irrational as a useful route to a new mental continent. For Artaud, bereft of the hope that he was traveling anywhere, it was the terrain of his martyrdom."[4]

To this one must add that constitutionally Artaud was a combination of director and loner who could only briefly and provisionally work with a group. Much of his failure to make any kind of theater he could respect work was determined by his isolation and poverty. Success demanded extensive collaboration and real funds. While the Alfred Jarry Theater put on four productions between 1927 and 1929 — Dadaesque skits and plays with no sets, stressing hallucinations and rude confrontations — they were interrupted and heckled by the Surrealists, reviews were mixed at best, and each production was a financial loss. While Artaud continued to act in films sheerly for money, he did not act on stage again until 1935, when his adaptation of *The Cenci* was performed, with disastrous results, seventeen times. All in all, he directed six plays and performed in twenty-two.

Artaud's most important work, as a Surrealist, is his film scenario, *The Seashell and the Clergyman,* filmed by Germaine Dulac in 1927, without Artaud's participation. As the first of the Surrealist films — followed by Buñuel's *The Andalusian Dog* and *The Age of Gold* — it centers on the metamorphic image of a seashell, exploring via abrupt cuts and juxtapositions the claustrophobic atmosphere of repressed sexual desire generated by a clergyman and an idealized woman. The anti-narrative structure is realistically dreamlike in its jolting, illogical sequences. Artaud actually wrote fifteen film scenarios,[5] of which, along with *The Seashell, The Butcher's Revolt* is the most extraordinary. In the latter work, bits of sound are percussively imposed out of sync with the visual action.

The failure of the Alfred Jarry Theater to become an ongoing venture ended Artaud's first attempt to affect French theater. However, his visit to the Balinese Dance Theater in Paris (1931) revitalized and transformed his ideas about what a theater might be. The Balinese emphasis on precise, subtle and ritualistic gestures (creating the atmosphere, as he put it, "of an exorcism which made the audience's demons flow") was to affect Artaud for the rest of his life. It also began to fill in his void with rich fantasy material. As he put it in his essay, "On the Balinese Theater":

> This perpetual play of mirrors which goes from a color to a gesture and from a cry to a movement, is constantly leading us over paths that are steep and difficult for the mind, and plunging us into that state of uncertainty and ineffable anguish which is the domain of poetry.
>
> From these strange gestures of hands that flutter like insects in a green evening, there emanates a kind of horrible obsession, a kind of inexhaustible mental ratiocination, like a mind desperately trying to find its way in the maze of its unconscious.
>
> And it is much less matters of feeling than of intelligence that this theater makes palpable for us and surrounds us with concrete signs.[6]

Drawing also upon Lucas van Leyden's painting "The Daughters of Lot" (calamity, incest, metaphysicality) and two Marx Brothers films (hilarity and anarchy), Artaud began to lay the groundwork for a theater that would function as a total art form. Dialogue, psychology, all sense of entertainment (escape from life) were refused; even the playwright was jettisoned, with the director becoming the "unique Creator." The theater was to be on the scale of, and up to, life itself — thus the title of Artaud's now famous and influential collection of essays and manifestoes: *The Theater and Its Double* (1938).

The concept of the "double" here is complex. It is not only life itself, but specifically the plague (to which Artaud compared his theater-to-be, sensing in both forces creative upheaval and renewal). Effective acting also involves the double: the actor is to become "an eternal ghost radiating affective powers." The double redoubles, so to speak, throughout Artaud's life and work, and ultimately becomes a kind of surrogate for Artaud himself as "Artaud the Mômo," the carnally-obsessed reviler homunculus who rises out of the ashes of electroshock at Rodez.

To the "double," as a crucial Artaud word, one must add "cruelty." Artaud's concept of a "theater of cruelty" did not mean a physical assault on actors or audience, but rather the steely rigor and dramatic intensity with which a "spectacle" would be carried out. While no Theater of Cruelty performance, on a grand scale, ever occurred, by 1933 Artaud had conceived of a potential presentation: the Conquest of Mexico — a cataclysmic historical event crammed into a time and space frame that could rivet an audience with its annihilatory grandeur. Such could obviously not take place on the traditional stage. Stephen Barber details the kind of spectacle Artaud envisioned:

> Artaud's innovations were aimed at every aspect of the theatre space, the actor's work and the spectator. He wanted to create new musical instruments to reinforce the aural dimension of his spectacle. These instruments would produce strange vibrations and extremely loud noise. The lighting would be like "arrows of fire." The entire spacial volume of the performance space would be explored; the barrier between the stage and the spectator would be obliterated, in order to facilitate a "direct communication" between the spectator and the spectacle. The spectator's viewing position would be reversed; the action would take place around the edges of the building, and the spectators would be placed in the centre, on revolving chairs. A central space was to be reserved only for the most important points of convergence in the spectacle's action. The building (rather than a theatre) in which the performance would take place would be bare, undec-

orated. The actors, in spectacularly exaggerated costumes, would have to carry all the spectator's attention. For Artaud, the actor would function as the skilled instrument of the director's intention, thus able to articulate intricate physical states. At the same time, Artaud was willing to allow the introduction of an unstable element of chance, whereby the actor's power of gestural metamorphosis could transform him back from an instrument to an individual. In all, Artaud's concepts amounted to an attack on the spectator as well as on the stability of the theatre as an institution. His audience was still an unknown quantity. The Theatre of Cruelty would necessarily generate its own audience: "First, the theater must exist." 7

Artaud's first manifesto for the Theater of Cruelty appeared in the NRF in 1932 and was predictably met with hostility and noncomprehension. Not only was Artaud attacking the traditional spectator and the stability of the theater, he was also replacing language with gestures and cries, a thrust that struck at the heart of classical French theater. Such implied that all social discourse was suspect as an authentic communication.

The following year, in April, Artaud delivered his essay/lecture, "The Theater and the Plague," at the Sorbonne. By now the need to break down (or "liquefy") boundaries had begun to effect Artaud's presentation of himself. After beginning the lecture as planned, he abandoned his text and began to act out the plague. Anaïs Nin, in the audience, has described what happened:

... Then, imperceptibly almost, he let go of the thread we were following and began to act out dying by plague. No one quite knew when it began. . . His face was contorted with anguish, one could see the perspiration dampening his hair. His eyes dilated, his muscles became cramped, his fingers struggled to retain their flexibility. He made one feel the parched and burning throat, the pains, the fever, the fire in the guts. He was in agony. He was screaming. He was delirious. He was enacting his own death, his own crucifixion. At first people gasped. And then they began to laugh. Everyone was laughing! They hissed. Then one by one, they began to leave. . . Artaud went on, until the last gasp. And stayed on the floor. Then when the hall had emptied of all but his small group of friends, he walked straight up to me and kissed my hand. He asked me to go to a café with him. . . He spat out his anger. "They always want to hear *about;* they want to hear an objective conference on 'The Theater and the Plague,' and I want to give them the experience itself, the plague itself, so they will be terrified, and awaken. I want to awaken them. They do not realize *they are dead."* [8]

Besides acting to make money, Artaud occasionally took on writing projects that while not strictly commercial would probably not have engaged him had he not needed money. In 1933, he was commissioned by the publisher Denoël to write a biography of the 3rd century adolescent Roman emperor, Heliogabalus. The decadence, anarchy, and catastrophe that permeated the life and times of Heliogabalus played into Artaud's widening obsessions, stimulated by Hitler coming into power[9] and the threatening atmosphere. "Poetry is the grinding of a multiplicity which throws out flames," Artaud wrote in *Heliogabalus,* associating the emperor with poetry as well as with himself. One useful result of research on the book was the amount of material on the occult, mysticism and primitive mythology that he dug up, some of which was fed into the evolving concept of the Theater of Cruelty, and some of which not only stimulated Artaud's Mexican journey but surfaced in the mid-1940s as visions and practices he would attack. Artaud dictated the final version of *Heliogabalus,* initiating a procedure used in the completion of many of his key, late works. During this period, he lived in wretched poverty (unable to afford new clothes), with several failed attempts at drug detoxification. Psychologically, he wavered between deep depressions and exaltations over the spectacles he would direct.

Artaud's last attempt to launch his own theater was his production of *The Cenci* in May, 1935. He had adapted Shelley's five-act tragedy of 1819, and incorporated material from the 1837 Stendhal translation of extracts from the archives in the Cenci palace. An atheist and sodomist, Count Cenci raped his daughter, and was subsequently murdered, in real life by the Castellan of Petrella, who in Shelley's tragedy became a pair of professional killers. Artaud, in turn, made them mutes, and in his adaptation, it is unclear as to who murders the Count. Artaud associated incest with cosmic cruelty, and he initially saw *The Cenci* as the first demonstration of the Theater of Cruelty. He soon became aware that the adaptation was a fixed text and made use of the conventional theatrical mannerisms that it was the Theater of Cruelty's job to demolish.

Like Heliogabalus, Count Cenci was a spectacular monster with whom one part of Artaud identified. And his insistence on playing the Count suggests that he was already predicting his own destruction. It also suggests that he believed that he would be destroyed as someone he was not, as if the real Artaud was still an indestructible unknown. Theatrically speaking, these double murders (murdered doubles) — Heliogabalus hacked apart by the guards in his palace latrines, Count Cenci murdered with nails driven into his throat and one eye — terminate Artaud's relationship to French society as actor, director, and playwright. While he would briefly return to Paris after eleven months in Mexico, his true, or transformed, return will not take place until 1946, when he returns with an internalized "one man band" show of the Theater of Cruelty.

With the failure of *The Cenci,* due to insufficient funding and ticket sales, Artaud was finished as a person capable of raising money for avant-garde theater. For many in his situation, the options would have been to make a conventional move or to self-destruct through increased drug intake and malnutrition. Instead, Artaud decided to leave France and explore Mexico, a decision based on his fantasy that in Mexico he would not only discover a still viable revolutionary situation (one which would welcome his ideas), but indigenous ritual that would enable him once and for all to penetrate the dead crust of European society and engage the origin of culture. No longer capable of tolerating collaborators, he was also playing with sloughing off his European skin — as tattered as it might be it still proclaimed his identity — and seeking to merge with "the Red Earth," "the constant irrigation of the nervous system" that he believed "flowed beneath the Mexico of the Spanish Conquest, making the blood of the old Indian race boil."

✴

Artaud spent the latter half of 1935 trying to raise money for his Mexican trip and writing lectures to give in Mexico City.[10] He also completed the material for *The Theater and Its Double* (which would appear in 1938 when he was in the second of his five asylums). Before leaving Paris in January, 1936, he again attempted a detoxification, which he could not complete.[11] He also became infatuated with a young Belgian, Cécile Schramme, to whom he would become engaged after his return from Mexico.

While passing through Havana on his way to Veracruz, Artaud attended a voodoo ceremony and was given a small sword embedded with fishhooks by a sorcerer. Once in Mexico City, he gave a series of well-received lectures condemning Marxism, proposing a revolution based on fire, magic, and anatomical transformation, as well as praising his own attempts to "rediscover the secret life of theater just as Rimbaud managed to discover the secret life of poetry." As usual, his enthusiasm quickly became absolute: Mexico was *the* place in the world where dormant forces could be aroused, one of the two "nodal points of world culture" (Tibet being the second, but its culture, according to Artaud, was for the dead). In the spring of 1936, he arranged for a journey to visit an Indian community, choosing the Tarahumaras in central northern Mexico because he had heard that they were completely uncontaminated by colonial Spanish culture.

At the end of August, with a Mexican government grant, he made the 750-mile train trip to Chihuahua, and then traveled on horseback for a week across the Sierra Madre into Tarahumara country. Artaud's particular attraction to the Tarahumaras involved their ritual use of peyote, which he guessed might do more than merely decrease his pain (apparently the main function of the opium and heroin addiction). He immediately attributed superhuman powers to peyote, believing it to be at the core of Tarahumara resistance to colonialism and the Indians' ability to survive for hundreds of years in a barren wilderness. He threw the last of his heroin away upon entering the Sierra Madre, and for the next week suffered from withdrawal and dysentery. He was spellbound by the Tarahumara landscape which appeared saturated with hybrid forms. In a mountain, he saw "a naked man leaning out of a large window, his head nothing but a huge hole in which the sun and moon appeared by turns." In rocks: "an animal's head carrying in its jaws its effigy which it devoured." He came upon "drowned men, half eaten away by stone, and on rocks, above them, other men who were struggling to keep them down. Elsewhere, an enormous statue of Death held an infant in its hand." Such visions, taking place in the "sobriety" of heroin withdrawal, appear to be the most specific sightings that Artaud took away from Mexico.

At the Tarahumara village of Norogachic (six thousand meters above sea level), he was housed with the local schoolteacher who, being the region's government representative, was opposed to native ritual, including the use of peyote. Luckily for Artaud, a tribesman had recently died, and in order to protect the dead man's double, the schoolteacher consented to a peyote ceremony. Artaud had to wait twenty-eight days for it, and according to his essay, "The Peyote Dance," by the time the ceremony was performed, he was utterly exhausted, and feeling the old, terrible emptiness he had complained about in Paris a decade earlier.

While he was moved by the all-night ceremony, he also felt that its essence was eluding him. The peyote itself mainly made him drowsy. He decided that the significance of the ritual was contained in the rasping sticks carried by certain sorcerers. "The Peyote Dance" ends with Artaud preparing himself for a crucifixion which he associates with a conflagration "that would soon be universal." Given the approaching European destruction, Artaud's prophecy seems prescient, yet we must keep in mind that he had written, as early as 1925, that: "There is something which is higher than all human activity. . . this crucifixion in which the soul destroys itself without end." To find himself being crucified at the end of a Tarahumara peyote ceremony indicates the extent to which Artaud was still registering his angst in Catholic terms. This semiconscious Catholic captivity continued to spread below his life, as it were, and suddenly poured up through him during an identity crisis in Rodez. In 1943, he would state that not only were the Tarahumaras really worshiping Jesus Christ, but that Christ had bestowed peyote upon the Tarahumaras.

Arriving back in France in November, Artaud reconnected with Cécile Schramme, and after a temporarily successful detoxification in April, 1937, made the second of his three international trips of this period: to Brussels, with his fiancée, to meet her wealthy parents. While the relationship was doomed from the start (Cécile was also an addict, and her promiscuity infuriated the increasingly, vehemently anti-sexual Artaud), the Brussels trip was a typical disaster; at the Maison d'Art, Artaud departed from his prepared lecture, "performed," and after he had scandalized the audience (which included the Schramme family), the engagement was terminated.[12]

Back in Paris, Artaud continued to waver toward disintegration. He decided that his name had to disappear, and insisted that his account of his Tarahumara adventure be printed anonymously in the NRF. In another work of this period, *The New Revelations of Being,* he signed the work simply (or not so simply) as "The Revealed One." This move into prophetic anonymity also involved him in Tarot card interpretation, and the increasing detection of magical signs and omens everywhere. At this time he was given a cane that was supposed to have belonged to St. Patrick. Artaud believed that the cane had "200 million fibers in it, and that it [was] encrusted with magic signs, representing moral forces." In Tarot symbolism, sticks represent fire. Artaud had a metal tip welded to the cane's end, so that it would emit sparks as it struck the sidewalk. While he was beginning to orchestrate with sword and cane apocalyptic destruction in his writing, in his daily life he provoked Anaïs Nin to jot down in her diary: "The Dôme at nine in the morning. Antonin Artaud passes by. He is waving his magic Mexican cane and shouting."[13]

In *The New Revelations,* Artaud predicted the end of the world on November 7, 1937. Illogical as it may appear, he also decided that it was time to "wake the Irish up by making them recognize the Cane of St. Patrick." He arrived in Cobh, on the 14th of August, crossed Ireland to Galway on the western coast, visited Inishmore (the largest of the Aran Islands), returned to Galway and ended up in Dublin in early September. His activities in Ireland must be pieced together via the postcards and letters he sent to such friends as Breton and Jean Paulhan, the editor of the NRF. While still in France he had identified with Christ as a sorcerer-magician who fought desert demons with a cane; by the time he arrived in Dublin he had begun to speak with the voice of God. He informed Breton that the anti-Christ hung out at the Deux Magots café, and that Jacqueline, Breton's wife, would be the wife of his identity-to-be. He also predicted that England would sink into the sea, and began to cast spells on people he wanted to destroy. The spells were small pieces of paper, filled with curses and colored ink splots, then burned with a cigarette in order to wound the body of the recipient.

Down to pocket money almost from the time he reached Cobh, he managed to run out on hotel bills until, in the later part of September, he was put out on the street in Dublin, and instead of looking for a new hotel, sought refuge at the Jesuit College, which turned him down. A few days later, he was arrested for vagrancy and put in Mountjoy Prison for a week. When the French Ambassador's representative asked him his name, place and date of birth, he declared that he was Antonéo Arlaud or Arlanopoulos, born in Smyrna in 1904. Deported to France as an "undesirable," he attacked ship workmen who came into his cabin (he apparently freaked out when he saw their monkey-wrenches), and was put in a strait jacket. When the boat docked at Le Havre, he was taken to the General Hospital. It was September 30th, five weeks before his prediction of the world's end. For all identifiable purposes, Antonin Artaud did not exist.

*

Artaud spent the next eight years and eight months in five insane asylums. One of his acquaintances, Jacques Prévert, said that what he went through was worse than deportation to a concentration camp.

At Le Havre, he was held for seventeen days in a strait jacket, his feet strapped to the bed. Hallucinating cats and black men everywhere, he refused to eat or take medicine out of fear of being poisoned. He heard armies of his friends, led by Breton, try to set him free. He also heard an actress he knew being hacked to death in the next cell.

On October 16th he was transferred to Quatre-Mares, near Rouen. There he was officially institutionalized. He described himself as a Greek, and Christian Orthodox, who was being persecuted for religious beliefs. He gave his profession as a caricaturist. He appears to have written no letters while in Quatre-Mares, and since he had falsified his identity his mother did not locate him until the end of December. He did not recognize her. After five and a half months, she succeeded in having him transferred to Sainte-Anne, a hospital in Paris.

While in Sainte-Anne, he was declared chronically and incurably insane and held in solitary confinement. Jacques Lacan, then in charge of diagnosis at Sainte-Anne, told Roger Blin, the only friend to visit him there, that Artaud was "fixed," and although he would live to eighty he would never write another line (Artaud later referred to Lacan as a "filthy, vile bastard"). After eleven months, with still no precise diagnosis made, Artaud was moved to the much larger Ville-Evrard east of Paris.

At Ville-Evrard, where he was to remain four years, his hair was cropped and he was given an inmate uniform to wear. Because he was now diagnosed as exhibiting a syndrome of incurable paranoid delirium, there was no attempt at any treatment. He was also said to be graphorrheic (subject to continual and incoherent writing). In a willy-nilly way, he was moved from ward to ward (maniacs' ward, epileptics' ward, cripples' ward, undesirables' ward) seventeen times. The onset of the war was accompanied by severe food shortages — cabbage soup being the primary "starvation ration."

Reluctantly, at first, he began to see family and friends. Once back in contact with his mother, who was now nearly seventy, he wrote her long, pathetic letters begging for an amazing range of provisions. Euphrasie Artaud was initially only allowed to visit her son twice a week, but in order to bring him food on a regular basis, she obtained permission for a third weekly visit. She would often just stand and watch Artaud, shattered. She must have loved him deeply.

The young interns in charge of Artaud noted their amazement at the ferocious energy with which he would fight the demons that he claimed surrounded him day and night. They also noted that he was utterly harmless to other patients. One of these interns, Leon Foulks, fascinated by Artaud's recounted and mimed stories, asked him to write out an autobiography. Among its details are the following: he was still Antonéo Arlaud, now born of a Turkish mother. Before he was two, he had suffered meningitis. He was orphaned at seven. After his trip to Mexico, he had discovered that he was St. Patrick as well as God the Father, and he had gone to Ireland to find a cane with which to combat the "Initiates." The doctors at Ville-Evrard and his friends in Paris were all infested with Doubles who were Initiates. Because "they" participated in orgies and sexual spells against him, he was compelled to fight them ceaselessly. Antonéo Arlaud himself had been invaded by Doubles, among whom were Astral, Flat-nosed Pliers, Those Born of Sweat, and the Incarnation of Evil, Cigul. They often dictated letters in his hand, and continually spied on him attempting to steal his thoughts before he could make them conscious.

This last complaint evokes the 1923 Rivière correspondence in which Artaud protested against someone or something invading his thought process and robbing him of what he was attempting to express. What had changed was that what had been in 1923 an abstraction (or void, as Artaud would have said) had become a drama, with plot and roles, a variation on the Theater of Cruelty, conceived and performed by and in the mind and body of Artaud/Arlaud. In retrospect, it would appear that the beginning of Artaud's regeneration took place in Ville-Evrard. Although his thought was still being robbed, he was beginning to identify the robbers as fantasy formations. In this sense, he was beginning to apprehend them, since he was filling in the void with their names and strategies.

While in Ville-Evrard, Artaud wrote letters, new spells, and the autobiographical sketch for Foulks. He does not appear to have initiated any other creative writing projects. There were several more stages for him to pass through before his surge of creative activity at the beginning of 1945. One of these stages occurred in August, 1939, when he dropped Arlaud and announced that he was Antonin Nalpas. Nalpas was his mother's maiden name.

Concerned that her son would not survive Ville-Evrard — he is described in 1942 as having become so emaciated that he looked like a walking skeleton — Euphrasie asked an old Surrealist friend, Robert

Desnos, to find a way to have him moved to a more humane institution. Desnos had a friend, a Dr. Gaston Ferdière, who was head psychiatrist at the asylum in Rodez in deep southwestern France, in a zone unoccupied by the Germans. Life was more stable there than in the Paris area. Ferdière, who had met Desnos through the Surrealist movement, thought of himself as a Surrealist poet with anarchic tendencies and he was proud that critics had called his poetry "cretinous" and "the product of a moronic mind." He agreed to accept Artaud and after considerable red tape brought about the transfer on February 10th, 1943. At this time, Artaud's total possessions consisted of:

1 passport
1 paper knife
1 file

*

Gaston Ferdière's initial response to Artaud, filled with mixed feelings, appeared in 1958, as part of his article "I treated Antonin Artaud":

On the very morning of his appearance at the hospital, after waiting for the arrival of the ambulance bringing him from the station, I held my arms open. He threw himself into them, making out that it was a reunion with the dearest of friends, that we had known each other for 15 or 20 years. He mentioned a dozen common friends whose names I did not know, reeling off a long string of specious memories which I was careful not to contradict. I told him immediately of my plan to give him his liberty, restore him to Parisian life, to the world of arts and letters, and I took him straight away to lunch at my home. My wife made an admirable effort, welcoming him with open arms, allowing herself to be kissed by this repulsive-looking creature. It is embarrassing for a housewife to have a guest who gulps noisily at his food, mashes it up on the tablecloth, belches regularly and, before the meal is over, kneels down to psalmodize. I was soon able to calm him down by giving him back a little inlaid sword which I had just found listed on his inventory. You can buy them at any of the markets in Toledo.[14]

During the initial months of his three year and three month confinement at Rodez, Antonin Nalpas also claimed to be Saint Hippolyte and a pure angel sent to replace the fallen angel, Antonin Artaud. Ferdière said that it was impossible to discuss any point with him and described his condition as "a poorly organized delirium." For his part, Nalpas claimed that he was attacked especially at night by demons whose goal was to steal his semen and excrement. According to Bettina L. Knapp:

He would begin telescoping his syllables, indulge in verbal gyrations, make strange noises, change his intonation and the vocal range of which he was a master; speak first in a sonorous, then monotonous, and finally in an insipid register; whereupon he would break out in mellow and full tones. . . At other times, hours were spent in articulating words forcefully, injecting each syllable with a kind of metallic ringing sound; treating words as something concrete, actual beings possessing potential magic forces. For the non-initiated, or those unable to understand Artaud, these syllable-words seemed to blossom forth helter-skelter; for Artaud, however, they created a tapestry of verbal images and rhythms.[15]

Such information suggests that as early as 1943 Artaud had begun to experiment with the "syllable-words" that were to be set, in stanza-like sound blocks, into letters and poems, occasionally in 1943 and 1944, and then regularly from 1945 on. From the viewpoint of the late work, Artaud simply moved his workshop to Rodez in 1943. The crux, of course, is that the creative significance of such "syllable-words" is contingent upon the fact that Artaud had the truly extraordinary capacity to gradually organize and ultimately give form to the chaotic subconscious invasions through which the "clinically insane" are incapacitated.

By the spring of 1943, "Nalpas" had again become obsessed with God and was taking communion several times a week (at one point he is said to have swallowed 152 hosts). He would sometimes pray with, and at other times insult, the asylum chaplain. His humming and gesturing increasingly vexed Ferdière. According to Stephen Barber: "[Ferdière's] position was that Artaud was 'violently antisocial, dangerous for public order and people's security.' He believed that Artaud could never be cured, but that he might be returned to a more creative and socially useful life. For all these reasons, Ferdière took the decision in June 1943 to give Artaud a series of electroshock treatments."[16]

Ferdière would later claim that it was because of such treatments that Artaud returned to his literary work and became capable of living in society again. Because such claims have been hotly contested by a number of people, it is useful to examine the relationship of Ferdière's attempts at getting Artaud involved in art therapy and the five series of electroshocks he prescribed.

After the first series (three shocks), Ferdière tried some translation therapy on Artaud, giving him the chapter from *Through the Looking Glass* in which Alice meets Humpty Dumpty to work with. Artaud translated this (and later came to detest Lewis Carroll), along with poems by Poe, Southwell, and Keats.

In early October, Artaud, on his own, wrote a long poetic text, much of which was made up of the language he was inventing.

At the end of October, Ferdière prescribed a second series of twelve electroshocks.

After the second series, Artaud wrote a critical account of a story he had read, and worked out a new text on his Tarahumara adventure. All this writing, including the poem with invented language, was intercepted by Ferdière and his staff when Artaud tried to put it in the mail. Artaud appears not to have been told of this interception.

In the fall of 1943, Ferdière tried out some photography therapy, requesting photographs from Artaud with which to illustrate a nursery rhyme that Ferdière found interesting.

At the beginning of 1944, Ferdière provided Artaud with some charcoal sticks and crayons. Artaud made a few drawings (including one of his Havana dagger) which Ferdière did not care for, and the project ended.

In May, 1944, a third series of twelve electroshocks was administered (by one of Ferdière's assistants, never by Ferdière himself).

In August, a fourth series of twelve shocks.

In December, a fifth series of twelve shocks. All in all, Artaud received fifty-one electroshocks during this eighteen-month period.

From the first series on, the treatment injured and terrified Artaud. In June, 1943, his ninth dorsal vertebra was fractured, forcing him to remain in bed for two months, constantly dosed with painkillers. During a subsequent series, Artaud stated that he was in a coma for ninety minutes (three to four times longer than the typical coma following electroshock), and that before he came to, Ferdière had ordered that his body be dispatched to the mortuary. In 1944, Artaud suffered the first of a number of serious intestinal hemorrhages (Barber suggests that they may have been the result of Artaud's near-starvation in Ville-Evrard, and the first indications of his intestinal cancer which went undiagnosed until the winter of 1948, by which time it was inoperable). Throughout 1944, Artaud wrote long letters to Ferdière and Dr. Latrémolière (who administered and kept a record of the treatments), beseeching them, on what seems to be a quite reasonable basis, to halt the treatment.[17] While Artaud's fantasy life ranged, almost at will, through all of his activities during this period, the facts are that his vertebra was fractured and that he was genuinely terrified of the treatment. Whether or not the hemorrhaging is related is unclear. Also, by the end of 1944, his remaining teeth had fallen out.

Responding to mounting attacks on him, at first by Artaud and then by Artaud's friends, Ferdière in 1958 gave his version of what had taken place in treating Artaud. In brief, he claimed that electroshock was utterly painless and that Artaud had only received between six and nine shocks (in contrast to the documented fifty-one). He also revised and oversimplified the relationship between shocks and art therapy, saying that Artaud had received a few shocks and then "asked to read again" (which according to Ferdière led directly to his translating and writing and return to Paris).[18] It also might be pointed out that considerable disingenuousness is involved in telling an inmate that you plan to give him his liberty after having decided that he is incurably insane and a menace to society.

While the electroshocks and art therapy were going on, Artaud continued to work on himself. Right before the second series of shocks, constantly praying and dressing as a marine officer in donated clothing, Antonin Nalpas — to some extent pressured by Ferdière — became Antonin Artaud again. Such a "return" did not release him from his religious fervor for another year and a half. Apparently, to be Artaud again was not in itself sufficient to clear out the religiosity central to his upbringing. In the fall of 1945, Artaud decided that his rejection of Christianity had taken place on Passion Sunday of that year, and he wrote to Roger Blin: "I threw the communion, the eucharist, god and his christ out of the window. . . I decided to be myself — that is to say quite simply Antonin Artaud, an irreligious unbeliever by nature and by soul, who has never hated anything more than God and his religions, whether they are based on christ, Jehovah or Brahma, not forgetting the nature rituals of the lamas."[19]

On the basis of such an assertion, one might think for a moment that Artaud had become "normal." But in the same letter he also insists that his asylum release is being obstructed by the oceans of spells put on Paris, the earth, and Rodez itself, and that he continues to await two young women, his daughters Cécile Schramme and Catherine Chile.[20] Artaud's behavior, in fact, continued to fluctuate wildly throughout his years in Rodez regardless of his relationship to his creativity at a given moment. As late as the spring of 1946, when he knew he was shortly to be released, he was still blowing his nose in newspapers, spitting everywhere, sneezing like an enraged cat, and growling and hissing through his meals.[21] What is crucial to note here is that as this bizarre behavior continued, increasing amounts of his fantasy energy were being articulated, especially in a number of letters to the Parisian publisher Henri Parisot in the fall of 1945.[22]

It is unclear as to why Ferdière did not resume Artaud's electroshocks in 1945. Artaud later claimed that he threatened to strangle Ferdière if the shocks continued, but there is no way to verify this, or, for that matter, if it did happen if it had any effect on Ferdière. Perhaps the closest thing we have to an answer is that at the beginning of 1945

Artaud began to draw on his own, and with such an all-absorbing intensity, that it may have appeared to Ferdière that there had been a crucial shift in Artaud's focus from unacceptable misbehavior to a concentration on a creative project. If such a conjecture makes sense, it would of course give Ferdière a self-congratulatory reason for ending his torture: here, from his possible viewpoint, was living proof that electroshock worked! According to Barber, the seventeen-month period over which Artaud was expressing himself via drawing was the crucial bridge to the literary works of the final period. What Artaud confronted in working on large sheets of paper with pencils, crayons, and chalk, was his own destruction. In flurries of dismemberment and reconstitution, images of splinters, cancers, torn bodies, penises, insects, spikes and internal organs were projected and realigned. Significantly, at this time, Artaud was befriended by a new doctor, Jean Dequeker, who had just come to work at Rodez, who in contrast to the others supported Artaud's routines of sounds and gestures. Dequeker later set down the following record of watching Artaud work on a self-portrait at this time:

> I was present for several days at the drilling of such an image, at the savage hammering of a form which was not his own. On a large sheet of white paper, he had drawn the abstract contours of a face, and within this barely sketched material — where he had planted black marks of future apparitions — and without a reflecting mirror, I saw him create his double, as though in a crucible, at the cost of unspeakable torture and cruelty. He worked with rage, shattering pencil after pencil, suffering the internal throes of his own exorcism. At the heart of the most inflamed screams and poems which had ever emerged from his tortured spleen, he struck and cursed a nation of stubborn worms — then suddenly, he seized reality, and his face

appeared. This was the terrible lucidity of the creation of
Antonin Artaud by himself — the terrible mark of all the
enslaved horizons — launched as an act of defiance against the
poor means and the mediocre techniques of painters of reality.
Through the creative rage with which he exploded bolts of real-
ity and all the latches of the surreal, I saw him blindly dig out
the eyes of his image.[23]

Artaud also began to write in notebooks, which he filled one after
the other, and which over the next year and a half came to some two
thousand pages. Drawing and writing began to overlap, with words and
phrases spilling into and around visual images. At the same time, he
began to transfer his humming and chanting into written sound blocks
which he inserted into letters and entries. One is tempted to say that in
a period of roughly six months Artaud taught himself how to draw and
write again. But to leave it that way would seem to me to undermine
and reduce what was taking place. The Artaud manifested in the win-
ter and spring of 1945 carried in its train, like a glacial movement, active
detritus that had been accumulating not only for years but probably
back into the memory wisps of childhood and infancy (the recreation of
his family genealogy overturns his natural birth). The achievement was
less a rehabilitation than a breakthrough enabling a cratered psyche to
rise into view, still smelling of its multiple deaths (indeed, with its mul-
tiple suicide deflections), and proud of its contours, affirmatively ghastly
in its power to at once protect and organize its loathed and beloved
cores. Central to this display was Artaud's creation of the "daughters of
his heart, to be born." By reaccepting the paternal family name, he was
not merely reaccepting his father since Antoine had previously been at
first dented (as Arlaud) and then rejected when Antonin adopted
Nalpas as his family name. The rejection here of Nalpas too, suggests

that both mother and father had been internalized, or composted, as it were, to make way for Artaud's creation of himself as one capable of parthenogenesis. Iconically speaking, if Artaud had now achieved his own self-combustion, the daughters were his charred circumference.

By the fall of 1945, with the war over, Artaud began to be visited not only by old friends from Paris, such as Jean Dubuffet and his wife, but by new, young friends, writers and actors such as Arthur Adamov, Marthe Robert, Henri Thomas, and Colette Thomas, who had recently discovered his work. Such support was immensely invigorating to the reengaged Artaud. Ferdière was now willing to release him on two conditions: financial support had to be guaranteed, and a satisfactory nursing home had to be found. Adamov collected manuscripts and paintings for a benefit auction from such writers and artists as Char, Joyce, Stein, Césaire, Sartre, Bellmer, Chagall, Picasso and Giacometti. He also arranged for Artaud to move into a clinic at Ivry-sur-Seine, twenty minutes southeast of Paris. While the actual benefit only took place after Artaud's release, Ferdière was reassured, and signed the papers.

A photo taken of Artaud on a bench in the asylum grounds sitting next to Ferdière right before his release shows him in much of his complexity at this time. At fifty, he looks nearly seventy; the area around his mouth is puckered from tooth loss; he is dressed in a thick, ill-fitting suit donated by French Mutual Aid. Yet he appears amazingly compact and focused, a little dandyish even, with a vivid and interiorized gleam in his eyes. Ferdière's final diagnosis: "Displays a chronic, very long-standing delirium; for several months, there has been the absence of violent reactions, his conduct is much more coherent, takes care of his appearance. . . it seems that an attempt at readaptation is now possible."

On the evening of May 25th, 1946, Ferdière accompanied Artaud on the night train to Paris, where they were met by some of Artaud's young friends in the Gare d'Austerlitz at dawn.

∗

On his arrival at the Ivry clinic, Dr. Delmas — who turned out to be genuinely friendly to Artaud — said to him: "Mr. Artaud, you are at home; here are your keys." Soon aware of Artaud's routines of sounds and gestures, Delmas installed a large block of wood in Artaud's room, which Artaud would pound with a poker (which he had twisted into the shape of a snake). Several months after his arrival, Artaud discovered a spacious, abandoned eighteenth-century hunting lodge deep in the clinic's wooded grounds. In spite of its having no running water, electricity or central heating, he insisted on moving in, under the impression that Gérard de Nerval had once lived there. Delmas arranged for water and fire logs to be brought in daily. Artaud was delighted with the place. For the first time in his life he had an ideal — large and isolated — workshop.

After the ferocious discharge of energy in Rodez, and with no need to worry about support (the benefit auction was hugely successful), Artaud flowed creatively without let up for what would be the remaining twenty-two months of his life. He worked even more relentlessly than he had in the final year and a half at Rodez, scribbling and drawing wherever he found himself, in the metro, in cafés, in bed, while eating, etc. He generally traveled into Paris during the day and maintained contact with his young friends who found him awesome, bizarre, charming, funny, and avuncular. New editions of his books had appeared in 1944 and 1945; his writing was suddenly, as never before, in demand and much discussed. He was also back on laudanum and when that became almost impossible to obtain he shifted to chloral hydrate, one side effect of which was to plunge the patient into sleep, to the extent that Artaud would sometimes collapse in the street. There is a photo from this period showing him sitting on a bus bench, holding a pencil up vertically against his back, like an apotropaic Gorgon eye. At times, walking down the street, he would thrust a knife violently into tree trunks.

One of the young friends that Artaud prevailed upon to procure laudanum was the poet Jacques Prevel, who was wretchedly poor and tubercular. Prevel kept a journal of his meetings with Artaud. One day when they were together in Artaud's new quarters in the Ivry woods, Artaud insisted that Prevel join him in screaming. Prevel apparently froze. According to his journal entry, Artaud then said:

> "You will not leave this room alive if you do not answer me."
> And he stuck his knife straight into the table. So I started to shout with him. It relieved me, since I had been hearing him doing it for two hours and I felt the need to do it myself.
> "You have done something very remarkable," he told me immediately afterwards. "If we had been on stage, we would have been a great success." [24]

Artaud's final performances were either solo events or small group recitals with young artists he was close to and had coached for the occasion. At the end of 1946, his friends encouraged him to present himself publicly, as if to fully register his return. Artaud was offered the Théâtre du Vieux-Colombier for the evening of January 13th, 1947; he proposed a program entitled "The Story Lived by Artaud-Mômo," and prepared to read from the five-section poem "Artaud the Mômo," as well as some additional prose concerning the imposition of death by society on the human body. By now Artaud had conceived a fantasy of what had happened to him during electroshock; borrowing the concept of Bardo from the Tibetan Book of the Dead — the forty-day period between death and either rebirth or Nirvana — he determined that electroshock created a kind of Bardo state in which parasitic beings, mysteriously associated with human organs, had unrestricted access to the one in electroshock coma. Artaud stated that he had seen these beings when he was in his ninety-minute coma and thus, from his point of view, dead. Beyond his control, he had been forced back into life, as if into a rebirth, so that these fiends could live off him.

Nine hundred people crammed into the Vieux-Colombier for what turned out to be, depending on the viewpoint, a freak show or a hair-raisingly moving manifestation. Artaud stayed with his prepared text for the first hour, took a break (during which André Gide embraced him), and then returned to read his lecture on the imposition of death. He became flustered, dropped his papers, and improvised for the next two hours, sobbing and screaming between gashes of silence about the hell he had been through for the past decade.

In spite of serious disagreements, he had kept in contact with Breton over the years. While the two men were the same age, Breton had a tendency to treat Artaud as a kind of black sheep younger brother. Breton now attacked Artaud for having made a fool of himself, and told him that he was still a theatrical performer. At the same time, he invited Artaud to participate in an International Exhibition of Surrealism. As if to prove his hard-won independence, Artaud tore apart Breton's criticism, and, refusing to participate in the Exhibition, painfully but with certainty ended their relationship.[25]

At the end of the same month, there was a major exhibition of van Gogh paintings at the Orangerie. Probably in an attempt to incite an explosive response, Pierre Loeb — the art dealer who would give Artaud his only drawings' show later the same year — showed him an article on van Gogh by a psychiatrist who spoke of the painter in terms similar to those used by Ferdière to explain Artaud. Artaud did respond, writing "Van Gogh / Suicided by Society," a forty-page poem-like essay, in several days. Filled with deft evocations of van Gogh paintings and grinding comparisons of the two artists' betrayals by psychiatry, the work argued for madness as an honorable choice in a society devoid of human honor. Artaud also made his clearest statement about the origin of art and what he valued in an artist:

> No one has ever written, painted, sculpted, modeled, built, or invented except literally to get out of hell.
>
> And I prefer, to get out of hell, the landscapes of this quiet convulsionary to the teeming compositions of Brueghel the Elder or Hieronymus Bosch, who are, in comparison with him, only artists, whereas van Gogh is only a poor dunce determined not to deceive himself.[26]

Artaud's own drawings had undergone modulations since leaving Rodez. While he still wrote and drew antiphonally in notebooks, his large drawings now mainly focused on the human face — self-portraits, and the faces of his friends. Many of these works evoke the "X-ray technique" associated with Australian aboriginal bark paintings, in which an interior life is imagined as part of a creature's surface. Magnetized to the human face, Artaud took his vision of the human body in his writing out into the unthinkable: a true body, one that had overcome "the glamour that organs cast on man to bind themselves more closely to him,"[27] would become organless, all bone and nerve, "a walking tree of will." By eliminating organs, Artaud also eliminated sexuality and, implicitly, the possibility of doubles, demons, and parasitic invasions. This transfigured body is oddly similar to N.O. Brown's "unrepressed man," free of guilt and anxiety, as well as "oral, anal, and genital fantasies of return to the maternal womb."[28] Both Artaud and Brown end up here in a Christian fantasy: a resurrected body, free of filth and death.

Underlying Artaud's rewriting/reconstructing of the body is a head-on collision between Sade and Savonarola. On one hand, Artaud identified with Heliogabalus, Count Cenci, and Ambrosio (who rapes his sister and kills his mother in Artaud's adaptation of Lewis's *The Monk*). On the other hand, he insisted that all forms of sexuality should be abstained from (in a kind of "official Surrealist" way he would "expel" friends who had affairs or became pregnant) and absolutely believed that the practice of sex was vampiric and drained his body of the powers he needed to live. Freedom, if such a word is cogent at any point in Artaud's system, would thus be contingent upon total libertinism and total asceticism. This contradiction is somewhat understandable, in terms of Artaud alone, when we take into consideration the onslaught against his body and the fantasy structures he erected to be able to express his experience. It should also be borne in mind that Artaud's closest friends were women as well as men — several of his women friends loved him dearly. Underlying his ambivalence toward the other is a similar ambivalence autoerotically speaking. While he vituperated against masturbation, the creation of the "Mômo" in the poem with that title is implicitly masturbational, as if the double were issuing from the speaker's own body. Such recalls the ancient Egyptian theology in which Atum says: "I copulated in my hand, I joined myself to my shadow and spurted out of my own mouth. I spewed forth as Shu and spat forth as Tefnut."[29]

In November, 1947, Artaud received an invitation from Fernand Pouey, a Director at Radiodiffusion Française, to prepare a program for a new series called *La voix des poètes*. He was to be allowed complete freedom in regard to his choice of texts, and he could choose the readers. He also had at his disposal a xylophone, drums, kettledrums, and gongs. He quickly assembled the radio poem *To have done with the judgment of god* (a title with massive vibration, coming as it did at the end of the Second World War), reworking material on the peyote ritual and writing several new sections preoccupied with the hopeless vulnerability of the given human body and the necessity to reconstruct it. With only one reading, and no rehearsals, the five-section text was recorded with three actors and Artaud himself (reading the first and final sections). On February 1, the day before the program was to be broadcast, Wladimir Porché, Pouey's boss, listened to it, found it obscene, and banned it. While Pouey assembled a jury of cultural figures who unanimously supported the broadcast, Porché refused to lift the interdiction. The portion of the text that had been taped, along with newspaper articles the controversy inspired, was published in April, 1948, shortly after Artaud's death.

Artaud regarded *To have done* as "a grinding-over of the Theater of Cruelty," and its rejection hurt him deeply. He believed that what the poem addressed was universal, and he wanted working people to hear it, under the impression that the pain and oppression it engaged was theirs, and that they would understand it.

A few days later, a doctor who had examined Artaud informed a close friend that he had a longstanding and inoperable intestinal cancer. Although Artaud himself was not informed, he seemed to be aware of the situation. While he now declared that he had said everything that he had to say, he kept on writing until the last days of his life. His final fragment reads:

> And they have pushed me over
> into death,
> where I ceaselessly eat
> cock
> anus
> and caca
> at all my meals,
> all those of THE CROSS.[30]

Artaud's body was discovered by the Ivry gardener who brought him his breakfast on the morning of March 4th. Artaud was seated at the foot of the bed, holding his shoe. Because he had been taking unregulated amounts of chloral hydrate, there was the possibility of suicide. This eliminated a Catholic burial service. Artaud's remains today are at the Saint Pierre cemetery in Marseilles, not far from where he was born, under a large stone cross. The sole inscription reads: "Family of Antonin Artaud."

*

While Artaud cannot be called a shaman, there is a shamanic resem blance binding his life and work. This presence contributes significantly to the way his image strikes us. While there is nothing in Artaud's materials, to my knowledge, that would indicate that he consciously made use of shamanic lore or stance, this lack makes the resemblance more pertinent. "Resemblance" is too vague: yet vagueness is of the essence here. When I hold up Artaud's image, I see shamanic elements in it, like a black rootwork suspended, coagulated yet unstable, in liquid.

Shamanic quest, initiation, and practice often involve the following:[31] a spiritual crisis as a youth during which the novice appears crazed or dead. Such a crisis can lead to a vision quest, which can be prolonged and excruciating. To gain access to invisible powers, the novice must undergo a transformation involving suffering, symbolic death and resurrection. Sometimes both crisis and transformation are initiated by forces over which the novice has no control: lightning or epileptic seizure. In other cases, psychotomimetic plants are ingested as "bridges" to the supernatural world. In the trance state of initiational torture the novice's body is "dismembered," sometimes "cooked," and replaced by a "new body," with quartz crystals instead of intestines. Such crystals are associated with lightning. One definition of a shaman is that he is one whose body is "stuffed with solidified light." The novice also learns a new language which he will intone to invoke spirit allies (or dispel spirit enemies), and he often takes on a new name.

Once a shaman, his (or her) work is to maintain the spiritual equilibrium of his community, keeping open communication between the three cosmic zones: earth, sky, and underworld. He facilitates this via the *axis mundi,* or World Tree, located at the center.[32] The World Tree appears in many guises: ladder, bridge, vine, stairs, etc. The long and dangerous excursions to sky or underworld — to retrieve lost souls or to accompany the recently dead — involve rhythmic chanting and drumming. The shaman's drum, thought of as his horse, carries him to the center and also helps him drive away demons. Besides his drum, his paraphernalia includes a staff marked with ancestral figures. During trance, he may speak in tongues, babble, or prophesy in a falsetto voice. He is sometimes androgynous and often prey to paranoid erotomania. He spits and gestures to discharge illnesses and spells attacking his body.

In the case of Artaud, a shamanic pattern, in a somewhat crazy-quilt way, is there, from teenage crisis, complaints throughout the 1920s of being nonexistent, a vision quest to the Tarahumaras (several decades before Carlos Castaneda popularized such journeys), use of a magic dagger and cane, the loss of self-identity and the possession by doubles and demons. To all of this we must add Artaud's subjection to a particularly pernicious kind of twentieth-century lightning, electroshock, during one seizure of which he was thought to have died. "Dismembered" in Bardo comas by battalions of hungry ghosts, he returned, semi-invented, with a new language composed of incantation and brilliant, if paranoid, argument, suggesting a lower and a higher register or a kind of vertical, vocal writing. He bore, out of his heart, a new progeny of warrior-daughters who became his assaulted messengers and saviors. He used the block of wood that Dr. Delmas placed in his room like a drum. He also had a "bridge" which he wrote was located between his anus and his sex, and it was upon that bridge that he was murdered by God who pounced on him in order to sack his poetry. Spitting, a falsetto voice (in his part of the recording of *To have done with the judgment of god*), and sexual consternation were also present. His envisioned organless body was an unsolvable problem because the lightning that destroyed "the old Artaud" (burying him in his own toothless gum) did not provide new quartz organs, or chunks of solidified light.

What is devastatingly missing in this shaman scenario is a community. On this level, Artaud is a Kafka man, put through a profound and transfiguring ritual while finding out, stage by stage, that it no longer counts. The Theater of Cruelty he pours himself into is ultimately truly cruel because the ceremony itself — what I would call the imaginative design of Artaud's madness — means little to anyone but Artaud.

Artaud is a shaman in a nightmare in which all the supporting input from a community that appreciates the shaman's death and transformation as an aspect of its own wholeness is, instead, handed over to mockers who revile the novice at each stage of his initiation. One might object here that Artaud was closely attended by a small but cultic group of friends in his last years, and that since his death his aura has continued to spread. The contemporary Japanese dance called Butoh looks like something he planned.

Such, however, is peanuts relative to the price of the loss of a functional community. Artaud ends up as an adored pariah, having literally failed in all his projects and performances. Robert Duncan wrote perceptively in the late 1950s that "we can entertain what [Artaud] suffered."[33] At first, I heard "we can be entertained by what Artaud suffered," which may strike a deeper, and more unnerving chord than Duncan's actual words. Certainly, Artaud enables us to entertain — reflect on — a level of suffering and fantasy response to that suffering that has been traditionally repressed in the art of poetry. That in itself is a unique achievement, as unique as van Gogh's writhing olive trees. But one fears that relative to the infernal combustion of the work the reader today is at such a remove as to put Artaud at the center of the bullring and himself in the bleachers. The burden of this introduction is to illustrate the terrible congruity of Artaud's life and work in such a way that any entertainment point of view is undermined. And to also argue that at moments the fumes emanating from Artaud's pit separate to reveal, in the depths, those regal and leprous lineaments of shamanic transformation that are the heart of poetry.

✳

Dead now for nearly fifty years, Artaud's power to fascinate, even mes-
merize, has not abated. His position in international modernism is
fixed, and while some casual readers still dismiss him as a psychotic
masquerading as a visionary, my feelings are that within the next
decade, as the full range of his writings and drawings become available,
such dismissals will taper off. Here we should keep in mind that there
has not yet been a major exhibition of the drawings in the U.S.
(although one is being planned by The Museum of Modern Art in New
York), and that our knowledge of his writing, at least in translation, is
at this point still confined to less than half of his published work.

Americans know Artaud for the most part through two antholo-
gies. Jack Hirschman's *Artaud Anthology* (1965) was translated mainly
from magazines and limited editions at a time in which only the first
two Gallimard volumes of the *Complete Works* were available. Helen
Weaver's *Antonin Artaud / Selected Writings* (1976), in many ways an
advance over the earlier anthology, drew on volumes I-XIII of the
Complete Works, and while it contains some of the key post-Rodez
poems, is weighted in such a way that Artaud's significance is posited as
a writer of prose poems, theater essays and manifestoes, and letters. In
effect, the Weaver anthology proposes that Artaud's importance lies in
pre-Rodez work.

With Stephen Barber's critical biography *Blows and Bombs* (1993),
and the continuing publication by Gallimard of volume after volume of
Rodez and post-Rodez writing, the shape of Artaud's body of work has
radically altered. As Barber writes: "The last phase of Artaud's work, in
particular, has suffered from a certain marginalization. It is the work of
a man newly released from nine years in five successive asylums, and
has sometimes been dismissed summarily. But this last phase is far from
a psychosis-induced linguistic stalling. More than any other phase of

Artaud's work, that from the period after his release from Rodez conveys a magnificent lucidity and lust for life. Utterly stubborn in its torrent of invective and denunciation, it is immensely versatile in terms of its imagery of the body, and in its linguistic experiments."

This is not to downplay the significance of such 1930s works as *The Theater and Its Double;* rather, it is to propose that Artaud has two major periods, with the shorter second period (1945-1948) containing more material than the entire first period (1923-1938). In the fall of 1994, Gallimard brought out Volume XXVI, and there are still more to come. There are now two major projects facing future Artaud translators: the 300-page *Suppôts et suppliciations* (Volume XIV presented in two books), which Artaud considered to be his summational work; and the *Cahiers de Rodez* (Volumes XV-XXI), over two thousand pages, worked at daily throughout Artaud's recovery period in Rodez. There are also four volumes of notebook material from Artaud's last two years in Paris.

This present translation attempts to do several things: to present very carefully worked (over twenty years) versions of what at this point appear to be Artaud's major poems and to present some of these translations (for the first time) bilingually, enabling the reader with some French to do an "on site" inspection of the work. By adding to these poems two seminal letters, a short essay on his drawings, and a prose poem and some dictations from *Suppôts et suppliciations,* we hope to be offering an accurate image of Artaud in his hybrid manifestations. As the one responsible for the final versions, my aim is to be resolutely accurate, on one hand, and, on the other, to attempt to match Artaud's challenging language performance whenever possible. Artaud is a translator's dream — and nightmare. One is always scrambling for new solutions that when found seem to add something unique to American-English. Occasionally, the combination of puns and coined words are such that one ends up not simply throwing in the towel but eating it: something semi-translated in the text and then commented on in the Notes that follow.

*

In our exploded and massively wallpapered age, I have found that in Artaud the ancient, black springs of poetry are graspable, like a writhing piece of star gristle. Antonin Artaud is the stamina of poetry to enact in a machine-gunned hearth the ember of song.

Notes to the Introduction

1   I am extremely indebted to Stephen Barber's *Blows and Bombs* (Faber and Faber, 1993), Thomas Maeder's *Antonin Artaud* (Plon, 1978), and Helen Weaver's *Antonin Artaud/Selected Writings,* with a fine Introduction by Susan Sontag, and Notes by Sontag and Don Eric Levine (Farrar, Straus and Giroux, 1976) for much of the material in this Introduction. To varying degrees, I have also made use of Ronald Hayman's *Artaud and After* (Oxford, 1977), Bettina L. Knapp's *Antonin Artaud/Man of Vision* (Avon, 1971), Naomi Greene's *Antonin Artaud: Poet Without Words* (Simon & Schuster, 1970), Martin Esslin's *Antonin Artaud* (Calder, 1976), and Charles Marowitz's *Artaud at Rodez* (Boyars, 1977).

2   Barber, p. 64.

3   Weaver, p. 70.

4   Weaver, from the Sontag Introduction, pp. XXVI-XXVII.

5   Several of these scenarios are translated in Tulane Drama Review #33 (Fall, 1966).

6   Weaver, p. 223.

7   Barber, pp. 54-55.

8   Hayman, pp. 89-90. Lest the reader get the impression that Nin's view of Artaud was shared by everyone at the time, here are Jean-Louis Barrault's impressions of Artaud in 1932:

> He had an extraordinary forehead that he always thrust in front of him as if to light his path. From this magnificent brow sheaves of hair sprouted. His piercing blue eyes sank into their sockets as if in that way they could scrutinize further. The eyes of a rapacious bird — an eagle. His thin pinched nose quivered incessantly. His mouth, like the whole of Artaud, preyed upon itself. His spine was bent like a bow. His lean arms with their long hands, like two twisted forked trunks, seemed to be trying to plough up his belly. His voice, rising up from his innermost caverns, bounded toward his head with such rare force that it was dashed against the sounding board of his forehead. It was both sonorous

and hollow, strong yet immediately muted. He was essentially an aristocrat. Artaud was a prince. (Hayman, pp. 81-82)

9   Artaud claims to have met Hitler in Berlin in 1932 (see Barber, pp. 50-51). In 1943, he dedicated a copy of *The New Revelations of Being* to Hitler (see *Artaud Anthology,* City Lights, 1965, p. 105). See also Invisible City magazine #6, 1972, in which Hirschman offers additional material on this dedication. In 1946, in a piece called "The Theater and Anatomy" (tr. by Hirschman in the issue of Invisible City), Artaud wrote:

> For since 1918 who — and this isn't for the theater — has tossed you a depth-charge "in all the lower depths of accident and chance" if not Hitler, that impure Moldavian of the race of innate monkeys.
> Who appears in the scene with a belly full of red tomatoes, polished with dirt like a parsley of garlic, who with bites of rotating saws has drilled himself into the human anatomy because room was let to him in all the scenes of a theater that was born dead.
> Who declared the theater of cruelty utopian and went ahead sawing vertebrates into barbwired mise en scènes.

10 Artaud's Mexican lectures and writings are collected in *Messages révolutionnaires* (Gallimard, 1971). Weaver has translated some of this material in *The Peyote Dance* (Farrar, Straus and Giroux, 1976) and *Selected Writings.*

11 Barber mentions that in 1935 Artaud was taking a dose of forty grams of opium once every sixty hours (generally absorbing it in the form of laudanum — a solution of opium in alcohol). From what I can tell, this is slightly less than De Quincey's average dose. Molly Lefebure, in her *Samuel Taylor Coleridge: A Bondage of Opium* (Stein & Day, 1974) comments that both Coleridge and De Quincey took what "would now be fatal doses of laudanum, because it contained so much less morphine then than now, when the quantity has become standardized." It is impossible to say, without more specific information, what the effect of laudanum (and heroin) had on Artaud's imagination. Like Coleridge and De Quincey, he became addicted when he was young, and drugs were not used experimentally (contrary to the case of Michaux and mescaline). While Cocteau's commentary on opium addiction is of interest (*Opium,* Librarie Stock, 1930), it sheds less light on Artaud's life and work than does De Quincey's (see J.M. Scott's *The White Poppy,* Funk & Wagnalls, 1969, pp. 53-56). For example: "I seemed every night to descend — not metaphorically

but literally to descend — into chasms and sunless abysses, deaths below depths. . . The state of gloom which attended these gorgeous spectacles cannot be approached by words. . . In the early stages of the malady, the splendors of my dreams were indeed chiefly architectural; and I beheld such pomp of cities and palaces as never yet was beheld by the waking eye, unless in the clouds. . ." For Artaud, might there have been visions of a theatrical abyss? Glimpses of his cosmically-expanding Theater of Cruelty?

12 "Artaud's lecture was to transform itself into another of the outrageous, invective events that stretch from his lecture on the plague at the Sorbonne in 1933 to his final performance at the Vieux-Colombier in 1947. Artaud immediately announced that he had abandoned his prepared text. He then spoke about his journey to Mexico, his voice and gestures becoming increasingly hostile and violent. He also dealt with the effects of masturbation on the behavior of Jesuit priests, thereby causing a large part of his scandalized audience to leave the hall. . . At the close of the lecture, Artaud screamed and told the remnants of his audience: 'In revealing all of this to you, I have perhaps *killed* myself!'" (Barber, p. 88)

13 Esslin, p. 49. Nin understandably mistook the "Irish cane" for something Artaud had brought back from Mexico.

14 Hayman, p. 124. Marowitz also translates this passage, with slightly different emphases, p. 109.

15 Knapp, p. 180. Knapp is quoting from J.H. Armand-Laroche's *Artaud et son double,* Pierre Franlac, 1964, p. 58. I have not seen Armand-Laroche's book, but according to Barber, who has, Armand-Laroche had access to Artaud's clinical records at Rodez, and his use of them appears to be accurate.

16 Barber, p. 106.

17 Weaver translates three of these letters, pp. 423-432.

18 Marowitz, p. 73. Anyone interested in learning more about Ferdière's recollection of his relationship with Artaud in Rodez should look at both of the pieces in Marowitz, the second of which is semi-hysterical and extremely defensive. See also Barber's commentary, especially pp. 8-9.

19 Hayman, p. 129.

20 See my Note on "Fragmentations," p. 331.

21 Maeder, p. 254. Artaud's behavior described here did not take place at Rodez, but at Espalion, a village 30 km. from Rodez, where Ferdière installed Artaud in a hotel to see how he would do in a nonrestrictive environment. He spent a week there in the company of André de Richaud, an alcoholic writer who was also in Rodez. Artaud's behavior provoked the hotel proprietor to write to Ferdière demanding Artaud's removal.

22 Six of these extraordinary letters to Parisot are translated by Weaver, pp. 441-465.

23 Barber, pp. 114-115.

24 Barber, p. 128. Artaud was not without humor, and I have tried to bring out his playfulness, ringed with bile as it may be, in various passages in this translation (e.g., the passage beginning "And now/all of you, beings" in *Here Lies*). Speaking with Marowitz, Arthur Adamov commented: "In spite of all his illness, [Artaud] always had an extraordinary sense of humor; one of the people with whom you laughed most." He then tells a few anecdotes, of which this is one: "One day I remember, at the home of Marthe Robert who was a great friend, we were having a discussion and Artaud began to exasperate us by insisting that there were lamas in Tibet who were willing his death. I don't quite know why, but we were very irritable that evening. We couldn't really believe that he was mad and so we said, 'Listen, Artaud, there may well be people who want you dead, but don't tell us they're in Tibet! Don't go on any more about Tibet.' And then he was very angry and left in a huff. After he'd gone I said to Marthe Robert, 'We've really been stupid. We shouldn't have contradicted him like that. You see how angry we made him.' Two days later, in the rue Jacob, I came across Artaud, who suddenly burst out laughing and said 'You remember that other evening at Marthe Robert's house? There's never been such good talk this side of a Dostoyevsky novel.'" (Marowitz, p. 83)

25 Artaud detailed his rejection of Breton and Surrealism in five long letters written to Breton between February and May, 1947. These letters were published in *L'Éphémère* #8, 1969.

26 Weaver, p. 497.

27 See David Maclagan's article, "A Language of Flesh and Blood," Link magazine, Spring, 1969, p. 10.

28 N.O. Brown, *Life Against Death,* Vintage Books, 1959, pp. 291-292. See Naomi R. Goldenberg's commentary on this passage, in *Returning Words to Flesh,* Beacon, 1990, Ch. 2.

29 Erich Neumann, *The Origins and History of Consciousness,* Pantheon, 1964, p. 19.

30 Barber, pp. 161-162.

31 Material on shamanism here comes from Mircea Eliade's *Shamanism/Archaic Techniques of Ecstasy,* Princeton, 1974, and Weston LaBarre's *The Ghost Dance,* Delta, 1972. For additional material, see "Hallucinogens and the Shamanistic Origins of Religion" by LaBarre in *Flesh of the Gods,* Ed. P.T. Furst, Allen and Unwin, 1972. Maclagan also brings up parallels between the career of a shaman and Artaud's own life in the Link article. In *Technicians of Ecstacy* (Bramble Books, 1993), Mark Levy dismisses such a connection.

32 For a gripping, visionary response to the destruction of the World Tree, see Charles Olson's "Hotel Steinplatz, Berlin, December 25 (1966)" in *The Maximus Poems,* California, 1983.

33 *Derivations,* Fulcrum Press, 1968, pp. 89-90. The entire passage reads: "A man's fortune starts when his fortune is told. To demand a new threshold of excitement and to work there: eventually to be unsatisfied, or shaken or destroyd in excitement? this is when no composition appears. Artaud is torn apart by actual excitations which are intolerable to his imagination and to his material. Neither his desire nor the object of his desire can endure his excitement. The writing he has left is evidence of the area of endurance. And Artaud's 'charge' is higher, in an entirely other category, than the charge at which I work. Yet I am concernd. His art — in which we have intimations of what we call 'insanity' — makes articulate what without this communication we would not be prepared to feel. We can entertain what he suffered." This passage originally appeared in *Letters,* 1958.

ON THE CHIMERAS*

* See the Notes collected at the end of the book for commentary on each piece, and on individual words marked by an asterisk.

Dear Sir,

I have just read, in *Fontaine* magazine, two articles by you on Gérard de Nerval, which made a strange impression on me.

You should know from my books that I am a violent and fiery being, full of terrifying inner storms, that I have always canalized into poems, paintings, plays, films and writings, for you should also know, from my life, that I never reveal these storms to the outside world. This tells you to what extent I have always felt Gérard de Nerval's life to be close to my own, and to what extent his poems, The Chimeras, upon which you base your whole attempt at elucidation represent for me those kinds of heart knots, those old teeth of an acrimony a thousand times repressed and extinguished and of which Gérard de Nerval from the midst of his mental tumors managed to make beings come alive, beings that he recovered from alchemy, reclaimed from Myths, and saved from the entombment of the Tarots. For me, Anteros, Isis, Kneph, Belus, Dagon or Myrtho of the Fable are no longer those of the suspect stories of the Fable, but new extraordinary beings, who no longer have the same meaning and who no longer convey famous agonies, but those, funereal, of Gérard de Nerval, hanged one morning and that's it. I mean that a great poet's power of repression before Myths is *absolute,* but that Gérard de Nerval, as you have said in certain passages of your articles, has added his own transformation, not that of an illu-minee but of a hanged man who will always smell of hanged man. To hang yourself in the wee hours from a street lamp in a seedy alley requires torsions of the heart as the first fruits of this immanence of hanging. It requires the pangs from which Gérard de Nerval knew how to compose incredible musics, whose value does not come from the melody or the music, but from the bass, I mean the abdominal bass cav-ern of a stricken heart.

Unquestionably, Gérard de Nerval studied the alchemical Kabbala which as everyone knows brushed by the Great Work, but never reached it. Whereas the poems of Gérard de Nerval, I mean the pecu-liar sonnets of his *irrecusable* Chimeras, are on the track of the explosions of the Great Work which were and will always be the plunge of the power of being into the delirium of revindications.

> Three times they dipped me in the waters of Cocytus
> And always protecting my mother the Amalekite
> I resow at her feet the teeth of the old Dragon.

Here Anteros takes revenge on his mother, if he has her born with old teeth. Here Gérard de Nerval writhes three times against the obliv-ion into which "the monarchs of the gods" plunge him as if into a bath of vitriol. The line reads:

> And always protecting my mother the Amalekite.

Who then? It is known that the Amalekites were a race which believed itself sprung from pure earth, without any compromise with god, but which, after a time and by dint of merging with the principle of generative slime, wanted to find this slime again in the uterus in order to extract its progeny from it, and if there is something heroic in this "always" with which Gérard de Nerval keeps protecting his mother, in the very midst of his descent to infernal regions, one can also feel there, and this no longer emerges from the Kabbala of Myths, or from the Tarot pack of blades, one can feel there, I say, this contraction of the first dentitions, and I will even say this frightful dental trituration of a duty which is on the point of letting go and rebelling against filial bondage. For the Amalekite is known in the Bible for also being the first mother who wanted to take from the earth the innate principle of god, and in the most humid part of her own earth cavern, the uterus, to incubate it *as* her own son. And to resow at *her* feet the teeth of the old dragon is to plant roots in order to make her grow perhaps, but also to bring out against her all the teeth of a maternal breast in order to get rid of them. And it's not only a question of meaning. I mean that the proof of the meaning of the lines of The Chimeras cannot be reached through Mythology, alchemy, tarots, mysticism, dialectics or the semantics of psychurgy, but uniquely through diction. All the lines have been written first of all to be heard, concretized by loud, full voices, and it's not even that their music sheds light on them and that they can then speak by simple modulations of sound, and sound by sound, for it is only outside the printed or written page that an authentic line of poetry can take on meaning and there it requires the space of breath between the flight of all the words. The words fly from the page and soar. They fly from the heart of the poet who drives home their force of untranslatable assault. And who no longer keeps them in his sonnet except through the power of assonance, to sound outside in identical costume but on a base of enmity. — And this the syllables of the lines, of the lines of The Chimeras so hard to beget, say, but on condition of being again and at *each* reading, *expectorated.* — For it is in this way that their hieroglyphs become clear. That all the keys of their so-called occultism die out in the finally useless and ominous convolutions of brain matter. For they are not hermetic, these lines, except for whoever has never been able to tolerate a poet and through hatred of the odor of his life has taken refuge in pure spirit. I believe that the mind which for the past hundred years has been declaring the lines of The Chimeras hermetic is that mind of eternal sloth which always before pain, and in fear of entering it too close, of likewise suffering it too close, I mean for fear of *knowing* the soul of Gérard de Nerval as one knows plague buboes, or the frightening black marks on a suicide's throat, took refuge in the criticism of sources, like priests in the liturgies of the mass flee the spasms of a crucified man. — For it is the painless and critical liturgies of the ritual of Jewish priests which provoked the excoriations and tumefactions of the body of that certain man one day he too hanged from the four nails of his calvary, then thrown in ox manure as pork fat is given to dogs. And if Gérard de Nerval was not hanged at Golgotha, he did at least hang himself, on his own, from a street lamp, as the dress of a too beaten body would hang itself from an old nail, and an old hopeless painting pawned. And that is felt now in his poems, that these are the poems of a hanged man, hanged facing the criticism of being, and the captations of rituals. Hanged facing the birth of fables, and the sources of allegories. For facing each allegory or symbol there is a priest like Dom Pernety, as there were priests in the Middle Ages facing the excoriations of certain beings still never born and always to be born, and hoeings of the bone of pain from which, they themselves not born and in nothingness, but living off this pain as the first fruits of their future maturations, these priests have extracted the symbols of that so-called science *the abortionist* of alchemy.

For Gérard de Nerval would not have suffered from life if life had not been put in symbols, had not been *typified* in symbols, cut up into astral homunculi in cooking pots, and if these symbols and allegories of beings, made desperate and repressed by the *rituals* of alchemy, had not moreover been put outside semen, outside that seed of tumors and semen which in real life leads to syphilis or plague, to suicide or madness. — What is madness? A transplantation out of essence but into the abysses of the exterior interior. What is essence? A hole or a body? Essence is this hole of a body that the abyss of the circular mouth of the cooking pot has never truly made signify facing the impatiences of alchemy. Does any bone powder remain? Not even that? But something like a false syntax, the sluggish larvae of an antique syntax in the skeletons of our brains. As no axis remains from the tarots, only the images from a lightning-struck imaginative flowering. Not the flocculations around an axis tree, but the flocculations of a collapsed primaryism. The Tarots are the idea of a Number on which to make things rest, and there's lot more of the great year of the centuries since this Number like a tree of bad stock has been driven out of reality. And if Gérard de Nerval steeped himself in all of that it is his Chimeras which saved him from it. — I mean that The Chimeras cannot be explained by the Tarots, even seen as the internal game of an alchemical prefiguration of things, and the drama of all the figures which enter into this prefiguration, neither can they be explained by that dark parturition of principles which is at the base of Mythology, for the principles of Mythology were beings which Gérard de Nerval did not need in order to be.

✷

I have never been able to stand someone fiddling with the lines of a great poet from a semantical, historical, archeological or mythological viewpoint —

lines of poetry are not explained,

but as far as Gérard de Nerval and especially his poems The Chimeras are concerned that seems to me a capital sin.

For the first alchemical transmutation that is produced in the brain of a reader of his poems is to lose footing before history, and the concreteness of objective mythological memories, in order to enter into a more valid and more sure concreteness, that of the soul of Gérard de Nerval himself, and thereby to forget history and mythology and poetry and alchemy.

What struck me in The Chimeras of Gérard de Nerval is that Anteros, Isis, Kneph, Saint Gedule and the Prince of Aquitaine become new beings there, not like Titania, Julius Caesar, Romeo and Juliet or Hamlet, Prince of Denmark, in Shakespeare's dramas, but like unusual and marvelous machines of consciousness, beating anew with a separate life which seems to *precede* Mythology and history, and not, as in Shakespeare or other poets, to *issue* from them. Which means that far from explaining Gérard de Nerval through his sources which could, following Georges Le Breton, be called scientific, I shall say that history, Mythology and alchemy have come from this internal animistic current with which certain very rare great poets in history have wielded the power of being, and the creative emission of objects. And these objects all of whom are beings are named Anteros, Isis, Kneph, Cocytus, Myrtho, Iacchus, Acheron, and the Dragon. — Which means that far from seeing Gérard de Nerval explained through Mythology and alchemy, I would like to see alchemy and its Myths explained through the poems of Gérard de Nerval. Poetry is a magnetic innervation of the heart, which the being of Gérard de Nerval kept all his life a cavern, one of the principal transmitting caverns of a void where all poetry is remade. Not one of the poems in The Chimeras does not make you think of the physical torments of primitive childbirth. And I myself do not believe that the *science* of his poems came to him from his research in the domain of Mythology or alchemy, nor that the dialectical reality of the legendary characters he evokes can come from any point of view to elucidate them, to locate them within a metaphysical flight, even if one wants to *justify* them before perception.

The metaphysical flight of Gérard de Nerval's poems is not that of the great mythic fables nor of the symbolics, themselves moreover terribly evasive, though not evasive enough, of alchemy; I mean that for the alchemists the way of realizing the Great Work is negative, by its nature it escapes being imprisoned in an idea or a term and never evokes anything but new states or facts and thus far never produced and which cannot resemble anything ancient or known; and if each of Gérard de Nerval's poems is like the explosion of a being from the Great Work, it is, this being, much better and more rightfully so than all the conquests of *real* alchemy. Which, I believe, has never in fact existed.

For historically alchemy like the rest is nothing more than a primer of a now determined number of scientific abortions, a formulary not completely catalogued, and moreover which cannot be, but which becomes so when it's spoken about, of operations at which man cannot aim without crimes, and whose equivalents have been restored to us only by very great poets like Baudelaire, Edgar Poe, Rimbaud, Lautréamont and above all Gérard de Nerval. And in the alchemy of history they are only the now outdated cooking of the semantics of a ritual. The soul of the untouchable poems of The Chimeras cannot be reduced to it, they are forever impregnable and intact before the approaches of commentaries or the mind's dialectical *classifications,* they cannot be reduced to comparisons with realities or allegorical keys already known, tested and understood. — And they are not merely pure associations of words and music either. — There is in these poems a drama of mind, consciousness and heart foregrounded by the strangest consonances not of sounds, not in the auditory register, but *animated,* the Great Work of a metamorphosis of the very principle of action, an expansion outside the unknown of innocent consciousness foundation of the most incredible explosions of language that a human being has ever reckoned. I mean that Gérard de Nerval's poems are tragedies, and that one cannot speak here either of purely pictorial, fabulous or sonorous disorders of the imagination without passing alongside the moral passional tumors, the marvelous moral affective liberations, of all these swimming carbuncles of consciousness and which god, that forever sententious, understood and primary expert, of all the rudiments of the unfathomable uncreated, has not ceased to make swim. And these tragedies of a repressed humanity, and which until now had never been able to live, are the tempestuous protests of breathing, feeling, perceiving and suffering beings that Gérard de Nerval in his allegorical hieroglyphic poems The Chimeras has succeeded in *bringing to light.*

One must cease speaking of mystagogy or occultism in regard to Gérard de Nerval's poems, one must cease referring to a Kabbala of numbers, and their forms, to a historical symbolism of affective fabulations, to an already existent semantics of feelings and their forms, to a dramaturgy typified by others of conception and ideas. The problem of the immaculate conception has never been resolved in the Kabbala of history, and the poems of Gérard de Nerval have not come out of the Kabbala or out of history, I mean that they are absolutely unrelated to whatever has already circulated in alchemy or the Tarots, and that they break loose and spread nonparallelly to a symbolics, a mystique, and the Kabbalistic allegories of the monstrously false and criminal science of the Initiated, but contradictorily to this science, and to all the psychurgic keys of the tarots' conjuring tricks.

In Gérard de Nerval's soul, I wasn't there, but his poems confirm it, terrifying explosions must have occurred in the course of his contact-seizures either with alchemical science, or with the manipulations of the terrifyingly primary and *impulsive* symbolism of the tarots. The tarots use still *unfinished* and larval states of consciousness in order to calculate a science which rests on nothingness alone, a science which attempted in the tarots to precipitate the birth of a symbolism of nothingness. Now, nothingness is for poets and not for sorcerers, pythonesses, fortune tellers and magicians. Nothingness is this abyss of horror the consciousness of which has forever been waking up in order to go out into something to exist. A world of parturitions not apropos of something but of nothing, and of nothing from the start, because at the beginning the soul knows nothing, it is not and knows nothing. But there is always the question of it. The basis of the Ramayana is not in knowing what the soul is made of but in finding that it is and was always made of something which was before, and I don't know if the word "remanence" exists, but it expresses very well what I mean, that the soul is a watchfiend, not a warehouse but a watchfiend, who always rises again and revolts from what formerly wanted to subsist, I would like to say "remanate," to remain in order to re-emanate, to emanate while keeping all of its remainder, to be the remainder which will reascend. — Now, this soul, the poet makes it and he alone makes it. And I don't know if the word "drama" comes from Rama, who was a being hostile to Brahma breath, but I do know that the poems of Gérard de Nerval are beings, extracted from Nerval from nothingness not through the tarots, alchemy or history, but through that somber story which was his own story, the survival of his old heart, the permanence of an old heart.

*

But through this somber story which was his soul, held for ages by the tarots of history or the alembics of alchemy, let's not forget that Gérard de Nerval died hanged, that he hanged himself on his own from a street lamp in the wee hours, and that suicide cannot be anything other than a protest against a control and I really believe it is that of time, not on the side where time is the time that follows us in present life, but on that where present life rebels against the presence of eternity. This eternal presence of a beast in whose copious belly the tarots of history and the alembics of an outdated alchemy still live. — Gérard de Nerval suffered dreadfully from the tarots, from alchemy and from history, and far from believing that he drew the genesis of his ideas from the tarots, from mythology, alchemy or history, I would rather say that it was in reaction to the symbols of myths and the primaryism of the tarots that through days and nights he invented the miry bone of the effervescence of his poems like one repells a putrid cross, parallel to the invention of what is malefically called the holy cross. For it is his golem, I would finally say, which made Gérard de Nerval as it made all great poets, this being torn from a body of the present and which the minds of ancient history force by *god* knows what sinister magic to return in their filthy stories, while that of the past is dead as the past is dead and really dead.

No, nobody has ever come back in the past or in history, but manipulators of a criminal magic extract from the body of each great soul a good body, good for sweating in the horrors of iniquitous history where their *obsolete* life feeds.

Facing Mythology or the Tarots Gérard de Nerval found again his own sources and the stories of the great fables pale facing the bomb blows of Desdichado, of Horus, of Anteros, of Delfica, or Artemis. For these bomb blows have a double meaning and they are in my eyes hermetic only for the one who still believes in Hermes, psychurgy, occultism, or the mass of mystagogies.

For Gérard de Nerval's poems are very clear and there is nothing in all the poetry ever written which repels the obscure arcanum, the obscurity of occult keys, the obscurity of the keys inscribed by the jealousy (of the holy ghost) of the whole spirit on the *deficiency* of our carnal humanity, of this humanity.

The flesh of humanity suffers, of course, but it's from letting itself fall into deficiency facing the pain of clarity.

It has not deserved to be pulled out of deficiency, but the conscience it blasphemes resurges in little children.

But from time to time, I mean at long intervals in the tenebrificated space of time, a poet has uttered a cry to make the little children come back. And Anteros, Artemis, Horus, Delfica and Desdichado are these women, the souls of these little children, the beings born in the tumefying eschar of his heart of a suicidal immortal who come to bell their drama in the foreground, the tragedy of their will to clarity: To illuminate the insistent tenebrae as I would say if I were Mallarmé, but as I will say like the Antonin Artaud that I am, the insistence of these tenebrae which rise up around my will to exist.

The first of these tenebrae is the spirit, wanting to know the how and the when by date and reference of the cliffs and coastlines of the churning seas of *tested* geography, reference to this invented river of time of facts which flows away in time, reference to feelings already lived, collapsed and supposed, reference to an entire drama already framed and delimited by history, reference to tested conflicts or passions (snapped up by the coffin), dissolved in the coffin, and which the recoil of death has fixed, but which fixed are even deader than if the beings who had lived them were coming here to relive them in duplicate on the models of the past.

So it is that past spirit does not shed light on Gérard de Nerval, and that his poems do not shed light on myths, neither and jealously no light can be shed on them by myths buried in the past; Gérard de Nerval's Anteros is, as I have said, a new being who does not shed light on the story of Antaeus, for Anteros is an invented being, the cord at the heart of a new assonance which comes from the bottom of the present sonnet to jolt repressions so well macerated and so complex that their aridity is a new clarity, and their complexity the simple braid of a cord long retempered in the earth which invented it. — And this earth has 14 feet.

What is Anteros about? A rebel. And to know from where he comes in mythology, or history, is to dissolve and assassinate him. But to wield his drama like a sword thrust is to make him live.

To make live this incoercible insurgent who from the blade plunged in his heart makes a weapon against the inner god, spirit of the thrust which wanted, itself assassinated, to strike him, and which he will turn into a murderous thrust.

I return the dart against the victorious god.

But how to animate this drama, how to make it live and see it again in saying it.

Gérard de Nerval's poems have been written not to be read in a low voice, in the folds of conscience but to be purposely declaimed for their timbre needs air. — They are mysterious when they are not recited, and the printed page puts them to sleep, but pronounced between lips of blood, I say red because they are of blood, their hieroglyphics awaken, and one can *hear* their protest against a control of events, whose protester will not be a golem but a being who drives Jehovah away from god in order to bring forth Belus or Dagon from him, and from Belus and from Dagon extracts Gérard de Nerval himself, insurgent against the monarchs of the gods and who says:

Three times they plunged me into the waters of Cocytus,

plunged naked to make me forget, plunged foetus to make me forget, scalded three times in that genetic vitriol, where all the monarchs of envy, monarchs of the celestial spirits' eternal envy of man, plunge man to make him forget his successive combats as an incarnated being.

Three times they plunged me into the waters of Cocytus

and protecting all alone, alone in my stubborn beingity,*

and protecting all alone my Amalekite mother,

and why now Amalekite this stubborn mother of Anteros?

Because from the race of buried ancients, which ones? those who like the first Amalekites were lovers of the eternal earth, of the stupration of animalities,

for anima the body's breath was this magnet in the earth, the soaked primitive uterine earth, and which had no other love and light, than to love this attitude,

to be like the uterus an earth, which in the name of anima its breath transplants its animality into the air,

ama,* soul throughout all lethe,

Amalekithe, race of the soul which has never been able to forget the irascible earth from which it was born which Gérard de Nerval will make live again like Antaeus sprung from the earth.

I resow at her feet the teeth of the old dragon,

this end, it can be understood in another way.

It's that the race come from the sexual earth of the Amalekites, humus of death by humus of death, anal larynx of putrefaction, and which in history left the earth to enter into pure sexuality, no longer terrestrial through deliberately accumulated and compressed dust humus, not dust but beings animated with knucklebones, which left the earth, I say, to enter into pure sexuality, incarnation outside of the knucklebone, and to be no more than the humid hole which in its placenta of humid mud reswallows itself through humidity, liquid micturition of an adiposity, this race made Antaeus forget his origin from pure powder, from expansive and animated powder (which if it is always a little damp is so only through its dry nature which detached itself from the humid) and this Antaeus who for himself was himself Gérard de Nerval wanted to avenge him, pressed for time like me or like you, reader of the poem, narrator or declaimer, pressed by the exigencies of things, thrown down by the dictatorship of things that the monarchs of celestial fables have not stopped representing, he was taken and plunged three times into the waters of Cocytus and, without wanting it but provoked by the old forgetful atavism of his unconscious, he still continued to *protect* his treacherous mother, the Amalekite who takes her uterus for a being and who made of her uterus a god. And uterus by uterus she believes herself to be, and to hold in this prevent[ive] coffer the genesis of her son god.

(Here the story of the blackboard at Madame Guilhen's where I was progressing too rapidly and where I was assassinated and put into the second grade.)

*

Lucifer and his beings have got me.

It is the original sin not of beings but of god that I believe Gérard de Nerval in his poems accuses, affections, volitions, *impulsions,* repulsions.

FRAGMENTATIONS

Out of the cunt without the mother I will make an obscure, total, obtuse and absolute soul.

✳

Yesterday evening March 13th Yvonne's party.
Children of the quickening little stick.
The Etruscan clay pot.

✳

Being is that parasitism of the brain that I have begun *by daylight* in order to rid myself of god and his sbirros: the diseases, the night.

✳

Born gradually this unconscious that I had like the hardest of the hard before the coffin of my six daughters of the heart to be born:

Yvonne,*
Caterine,
Neneka,
Cécile,
Ana
and
Little Anie.

*

Before they got away from me I had already blasted them into a state more terrifying than that god they reached only later.

*

Bigger on this floor where the biggest one was hardening to she-death, not like a knee barded with a kneecap, but like the infinitely small that progresses into the angle of its sempiternal strangulation.

*

Which indeed is not in philosophy, but in the pan of fried potatoes, square perhaps and with the handle of the cantilever which bears like the spoon in the perforated tongue of the sex organ forever denied by the heart.

*

A dead little girl said: I am the one who bubbles over with horror in the lungs of the living. Get me out of here right away.

*

They blew terms of dead wax on the condemned bodies of beings and made stupefying retentions of them, who, before birth, were not, but who,
insulin by insulin,

were believed to be,

and yet the artichoke gets worked up in its stalk when a virgin makes caca.

Insulin it's Ka* without shit, shit without making caca.

✳

There are only the dead
asleep in me,
some are free, they are outside,
the others in this hellish dungheap where my thighbone ceaselessly goes forth and grazes in order to undermine hell.

✳

Yesterday Friday March 15th in the installation of my suffering, the dialectic entered me like the derision of my living flesh which suffers but does not understand.

✳

Morphine on a wooden leg, done, this morphine, with the gangrene of the dead leg's bones, then drawn off, here is what the
holy trinity was.

✳

It isn't enough to agitate fluids in order to explain consciousness which is not a common spirit but the volume of a body's timbre up to the point where it arms its way in in order to be, against the spirit that will *calculate* it.

*

Evil spirits are not mental states but beings who never wanted to en-dure themselves.

*

The spirits will not take care of my affairs and I will regulate them always with my hands and without a concept, like a worker adjuster of limbs whose principle is in my sperm box, and the coffins of my stake legs.

*

But once the stake is out, the question is no longer of adjusting limbs, but of making it, it, explode into a limb which does not suffer replacement.

*

For the children of the principle stage setting,
they're not in the sound, but in the cunt,
which is not the original granary of a principle but a terrifying chewing.

Not in the tone, but in the cunt, drastic bend of this ground swell, advancing with its horrible denture of beings, created to swallow up all beings, but who never know where they are.

✶

In slumber one sleeps, there is no self, nobody only specters,
snatching of the tétême* of being, by other beings (at that moment
awake), from that which makes one a body.

And what is the tétême?

The blood of the body at that moment stretched out, dozing
because it is sleeping. How can the tétême be blood? By the *éma,* before
which rests the t and designates that which rests like the té vé* of the
Marseillais. For the té makes a cinder sound when the tongue places it
on the lips where it will smoke.

And Éma in Greek means blood. And tétême, twice the cinder on
the flame of the blood clot, this inveterate clot which is the body of the
sleeping dreamer who would do better to wake up.

— For neither the unconscious nor the subconscious is the law.

Each dream is a piece of suffering torn out of us by other beings, by
chance with the monkey hand which they throw upon me every night,
the resting cinder of our self which is not a cinder but a hail of bullets as
the blood is scrap iron and the self ferruginous.

And what is the ferruginous?

It's this simple: a head, a trunk on two legs, and two arms to rock
the trunk in the sense of always being more with a head, two legs and
two arms.

For it has been said from time immemorial that the illiterate is a
mystery, without alpha and without omega, but with a head, two legs,
two arms. — The oafish illiterate of the simple which is man and
doesn't understand. He understands that he is head and arms, legs to get

the trunk moving. And that there is nothing else apart from that: this totem of eyelids ears, and a nose drilled by twenty fingers .

And that is the mystery of man which god the spirit has never ceased pestering.

*

There is no inside, no spirit, outside or consciousness, nothing but the body as it may be seen, a body that does not cease being, even when the eye that sees it falls.
And this body is a fact.
Me.

*

Sperm is not urination but a being who always toward a being advances to torrefy it with itself.

*

Not a fiction, this sperm, but war with thorn-crowned cannons which churn their own grapeshot before *churning* the ONE entry.

*

Operation from which man fell the day he consented to play the fool.

*

And 2°
secondly
it was not nails
but nothingness,
which one day proclaimed itself a nail,
because it had scraped my head too much and because I, Antonin
Artaud, to punish it for sucking my head I turned it into a nail with one
hammer blow.

*

I saw Yvonne's bloated sac, I saw the sac bloated with the dregs of
Yvonne's blistered soul, I saw that horrific soft sac of Yvonne's sodom-
ized soul, I saw Yvonne's swelling heart punctured, like an enormous
bloated sac of pus, I saw the corpse of this insulted Ophelia crawling not
on the Milky Way, but on the way of human filth, cursed, reviled,
loathed, I saw the corpse of she who loved me subjected to rancid
belches of the soul with kicks and slaps,

I saw at last the abhored bloating, the hideous swelling of this heart
plagued for having wanted to bring me a metalloid when I had nothing
to eat,

I saw it pass, this brown sac like the pus of despair, I saw pass the
dead goiter of my daughter whom life had seized upon to repell and
infect.

I saw her repell herself, bitterdead from having been so insulted.

*

I saw the corpse of my daughter Anie reduced to ashes and her sex organ dilapidated and divided after her death, by the police of the French.

*

Priests are asses* without egos who are endlessly talking into the asses of others in order to implant their ego there.

*

I saw the meningeal syphilis of my daughter Caterine's legs, and the two hideous potatoes of her swollen kneecaps, I saw the onions of her toes blistered like her sex organ which she has no longer been able to wash for a year after she began her march. I saw it burst from her skull like Anie of the "Holy" Throat, and I saw the intestinal crown of thorns of her blood flowing from her on nonmenstrual days.

And I saw the notched knife of my other daughter Neneka who I felt moving in the opium of the earth,

and there were also Yvonne, Caterine, Cécile, Anie and Ana with Neneka.

And she was the dental opium, for nothing is harder than a raging toothache. The opium of the earth's masticatory canines which everyone has been crushing underfoot.

She loved me when I was chewing one day in order to compose the earth, the earth which I will eat.

And I saw the human phallus, thrashing the breasted heart of
Cécile,

in that groove of a bone rack,

where the soul to be confirmed smells of a dead woman,

open mouth of an imperishable cellar.

For the offered blood smells of cinders in the casks of its cellar. —
And how many testicles of hatred have flogged this first-born heart?

There still remains Ana and Anie.

*

It's chance which is infinity and not god, and what is chance?

It's *me,* my me told me who listens to me.

And I answered him: All my selves have reached this stage because
as far as I am concerned I'm not listening to you.

*

It's Ana who loved the music one day from the top of that shed who
is listening to me, when I'm thinking not of myself but of her. Who is
she?

The soul that will be born from me.

All of this is very well, but when will I again see Ana Corbin across
whose belly the whole medical profession has passed, Ana Corbin
named a slut by all the petites-bourgeois tarts from Saint-Roch to
Notre-Dame-des-Champs?

Ana Corbin, first-born daughter of my soul, and who died despair-
ing of me.

Never!

Yes, one day, the day soon when I'll finally be able to eat.

$$*$$

And to marry me Ana Corbin will have waited for the earth to be cleaned, like Yvonne, Cécile, Anie, Caterine and Neneka, these dead, who beyond the distress of their limbs, are waiting before coming to me until I have got done marrying my Ka Ka.

$$*$$

There one would have to eat the earth, once.

$$*$$

And I have seen Martha Robert* in Paris, I saw her from Rodez to Paris leaning forward angrily in the angle of my closed room, right in front of my night table, like a flower extirpated angrily, in the apocalypse of life.

$$*$$

And there was also Colette Thomas, to blow the gendarmes of hatred from Paris to Nagasaki.
She will explain to you her own tragedy.

POST-SCRIPTUM

I had a dream last night, scrambled, yes indeed, for a scrambled dream it sure was scrambled. But so meaningful on the other hand, so meaningful.

Jean Dequeker* was dragging himself along the earth with short and truncated legs, and he said: Am I a beast, a pebble, a branch or a meat stall?

But after all what is a tree? What is a tree?

Madame Dequeker was behind a cage with her stomach pressed against the flange of this cage, saying: Is that my very own stomach,

no. . .

(me is it not my stomach?)

isn't it my very own stomach which will end up succeeding in thundering?

Colette Thomas had a face full of Greek fire and exclaimed: If that doesn't stop I blow.

Madame Dequeker, the old lady, was in the invisible, like the silvering of a puddle of being which would not succeed in coming back, with her right hand in the air and her left like an old membrane floating over her abdomen, and saying: I certainly would like my two hands to rejoin without joints, but no joined hands, no, no joined hands. — But how difficult that is, how difficult.

TO PETER WATSON

Dear Sir,

I entered into literature by writing books in order to say that I was unable to write anything, my thought when I had something to say or to write was what was denied me most. I never had any ideas and two very short books, 70 pages each, revolve around this profound, inveterate, endemic absence of any idea. They are *l'Ombilic des Limbes* and *le Pèse-Nerfs*.

At the time they seemed to me full of cracks, of faults, of platitudes, and as if stuffed with spontaneous abortions, of abandonings and all sorts of abdications, always traveling along the side of anything essential or big that I wanted to say and which I said that I never would say. — But after 20 years' lapse they appear to me staggering, successful not in respect to me but in respect to the inexpressible. Thus it is that works mature and that while all of them *lie* as far as the writer is concerned, in themselves they constitute a bizarre truth which life, if it were authentic itself, should never have accepted. — An inexpressible expressed through works which are nothing but debacles now, and which have value only through the posthumous distance of a spirit dead with time, and stalemated in the present, will you tell me what it is?

Since then I have written several other works: *l'Art et la Mort, Héliogabale, le Théâtre et son Double, Voyage au Pays des Tarahumaras, Nouvelles Révélations de l'Être, Lettres de Rodez.*

In each one I have been pursued by this sinister harlequinade of a well with tiers of texts superimposed one on top of another and which appear on one level alone, like the grating of a secret checkerwork, in which yes and no, black and white, true and false although contradictory in themselves have melted into one man's style, that of this poor Mr. Antonin Artaud.

I do not remember being born in Marseilles on the night between the 3rd and the 4th of September, 1896, as my birth certificate states, but I do remember having argued there with a serious question, in a place which was not one, situated somewhere between space and a world sinister, fortuitous, unliveable, grotesque, dreadfully inexistent.

Space led onto a ladder of lives where I saw no interruption to my being,

the sinister, dreadful, grotesque world was that of this particular life.

The question with which I was arguing was to know if I will go to a white charnel house, if, always tired of existing, I will turn myself over to that white center which. . .

or if I will remain faithful to that black water, to that aqueous lid of a cistern of black water, which was obstinately holding me back. — That smelled of shit on my heart, this cistern with my trunk inside, but it was my ego, the excrement.

In short the cistern was a bloody trunk, but the trunk of a man, while the white hole offering me its soul, a woman, was but nothingness to me.

Will I go to the mother or will I stay father, all things considered the eternal father that I was?

One must believe that I have chosen to be father for eternity, for I've been a man for 50 years now and I don't see that this could change.

For if before this life I have had others I do not believe that there will are others afterwards.

Death is not just a state of passage. It is a state that never has existed, for if it is difficult to live it is getting more and more impossible and ineffective to die, — looking carefully at this life I remember being dead in it really and corporeally at least 3 times, once in Marseilles, once in Lyons, once in Mexico and once at the Rodez asylum in the coma of electroshock. Each time I saw myself leaving my body and traveling through spaces, but not very far from my own body, for one is never very well detached. And in reality one never leaves one's body. The body is a trunk of which one is only a leaf when one realizes that one is dead, and that one is not outside but inside.

For the dead man has only one idea it is to return to his corpse, to take it back again in order to go forward.

But it is always he who takes you back,

and one obeys because one is inside.

So then the dead man is a being who lies, one must suffer still, now is not the moment, says the voice of dreaming conscience, and those who speak are they dead or living? — One can no longer tell. — Dead, I've been seized by the tornado of beings all chafed from hate, and demented. — This hate gave me an idea, which I felt going around in my absent ears, and which brought my hand back to my side. This idea was that each being had made me lose an event, and that death was merely a story that I should have lived living.

Dead, one dies on the wrong side, it is not the path that one should take.

Only, as long as I am alive, I don't believe in the path, and I do not believe that the dead believe in it or have to argue about it. We are not

dead really dead when we calculate this or that.

And that, dear Mr. Peter Watson, does it interest you to know how we are when we don't calculate, really do not. — And what happens otherwise than there, and whether we are or whether we are not there.

And I don't think that does interest you and as far as I'm concerned, for a long, a very long, a very long time it has ceased to be of interest to me!

Enough, enough and enough of questions and problems, of problems and questions, of life and thought, of death and the nought (and this rhymes, can't you see that it rhymes? Oh this life that never wants to go away). But then wait before thinking until you have at least something to say, Mr. Artaud.

No, I, Antonin Artaud, well then no, well then precisely no, I, Antonin Artaud, I only want to write when I have nothing more to ponder. — Like someone who would eat his belly, the winds of his belly from inside.

You say that the English public doesn't know me. And where indeed could they have picked up *la Correspondence avec Jacques Rivière, l'Ombilic des Limbes, le Pèse-Nerfs, l'Art et la Mort, le Moine* de Lewis, *Héliogabale ou l'Anarchiste couronné, les Nouvelles Révélations de l'Être, le Théâtre et son Double, le Voyage au Pays des Tarahumaras, les Lettres de Rodez,* and last and especially "Letura d'Eprahi," written in 1935, in which I put the best of myself, which has been lost and which I have never recovered although it was printed so magnificently in characters taken out of ancient incunabula,

no,

in characters of which the very ancient incunabula were only an imitation,

a duplicate tracing,

a castrated transposition of its own head,
and, excuse me for using bizarre, and somewhat pedantic, words,
but I will say a transposition

voctrovi[*]
cano dirima
cratirima
enectimi

vonimi
cano victrima
calitrima
endo pitri

calipi
ke loc tispera
kalispera
enoctimi

vanazim
enanzimi

all stupid incantations in a fake lingua franca, good for summoning
fake dead men
to say that after the printing of this book the world got the hell out,
and that before the first incunabula the world also had gotten the hell
out. For from time to time, dear Mr. Peter Watson, life makes a leap,
but that is never written in history and I have never written except to fix
and perpetuate the memory of these cuts, these scissions, these ruptures,

these abrupt and bottomless falls
   which

✳   ✳   ✳

but imagine, dear Mr. Peter Watson, that I have never been more than a sick man and I shall not go on about it to you.

I repeat to you, I have never been able to live, to think, to sleep, to talk, to eat, to write

and I have never written except to say that I have never done anything, could never do anything, and that in doing something in reality I was doing nothing. My whole work has only been and could only be built on this nothingness,

on this carnage, this skirmish of extinguished fires, of dried-up cries and slaughter,

one does nothing, one says nothing, but one suffers, one despairs and one fights, yes, I believe that one really does fight. — Will the struggle be evaluated, will it be judged, will it be justified?

No.

Will it be denominated?

No again,

naming the battle is to kill nothingness, perhaps.

But above all to stop life. . .

One will never stop life.

But one will come out onto the plain at least, I mean onto the terreplein after the battle. To sniff the memories of the struggle?

Never.

The struggle has started up again further below, so what? A scabrazage* for perpetuity? An infinite scraping at the wound. The infinite plowing of the slit from where the wound emerged?

Perhaps!

But you're mad?

Indeed not; and it is you who are only an imbecile,

I, Antonin Artaud, I'm boiling, I'm boiling, you, critic, you browse my prick outside.

And that is all that characterizes you, that stops you, and that makes you.

There where I am nothing has any more meaning and life is not, it is not at your lubricious low-water mark, you who love only what can be appreciated.

You have no tongue for eating or for speaking but for jousting, for planting the tip of your brain in the unctuous silt of the throe, and for stirring it, for making it stir like mayonnaise or aïoli, you have not made the throe which makes you exist, oh cowards, for you emerged from its pain, like fugitives, and it is on the cream of your flight that you have based life. — *To gauge* evil is this lubricious state with which you have made your metrical bow oar, your kind of calculated argot!

arganufta
daponsida
parganuft

ebanufte
parganupt
ebanupte
pelozipter

palon
petonme

onme

niza

All your great books from the Vedas to the Gospels by way of the Upanishads, the Brahma-putras and the imitation of Jesus christ consist only of this search for a happiness and a beatitude whose bottom is an erotic,

not love but an erotic,

the search for a *lacuna* state as a low-water mark of the infinite.

He who lives takes no rest and does not know if he belongs to happiness or to the Miserere,

to hell or to paradise.

He lives and that's it.

Music does not stir his flesh

(and the aioli contemplates you, spirit, and you contemplate your aioli. At last shit to the infinite!)

Contemplative states are the states of a lubricious buzzard, of astrayers of deeply grounded energy, of those with their *anomaly* circumcised.

The anomaly being the evidence.

The male is built on the strong anus, the anus is not a hole but the penis.

The anus ache being the sphincter, a suffocation which always takes a being who wants to live, and judges him, what? Yes, judges him according to his intrinsic capacity for suffocating this suffocation. For being before the tightening of the penis, the male of the most intense tightening.

But then that is bad verbal sophistry, all of it. — In reality the Jew is the one who from life and from being wanted to extirpate suffering as *li tigation** of existence. I say li-tigation. — What does that mean.

It means liege man and liege om.

Breath li tigation of death. Horrible delict of entering into being, without pain, so that it is no longer in tigation.

But that one should live happily off the dead, happily on the camphor and powder of the valorous corpses of the dead.

I am that dead man whose powder is eaten: thyroidal or ovarian extract of caput, of the end of when it's over

and I know it.

Of ghastly petits-bourgeois initiated into puckering their mouths into a kiss to suck in the departed soul, they eat my powder of a departed soul in this way night and day,

which is why I'm sick each time I wake up, and am sick all day long.

For there would be no sickness without vampires, spellbinders and initiates.

How well I know it.

I know from which abject centers these maneuvers set forth over all the earth, and *who* those millions are who, to live, have thus chosen to bask in the dust,

the dust of survivor selves,

the dust of myself, surviving.

And it was to shut my mouth that in 1937 in Ireland I was thrown into prison, then locked up and confined in France for 9 years in an insane asylum.

My work says much less than my life about all this, but it says it.

Very amicably yours.

ANTONIN ARTAUD

13 September 1946

ARTAUD LE MÔMO

ARTAUD THE MÔMO

L'esprit ancré,
vissé en moi
par la poussée
psycho-lubrique
du ciel
est celui qui pense
toute tentation,
tout désir,
toute inhibition.

o dedi
a dada orzoura
o dou zoura
a dada skizi

o kaya
o kaya pontoura
o ponoura
a pena
poni

The Return of Artaud, the Mômo

The anchored spirit,
screwed into me
by the psycho-
lubricious thrust
of the sky
is the one who thinks
every temptation,
every desire,
every inhibition.

o dedi
o dada orzoura
o dou zoura
a dada skizi

o kaya
o kaya pontoura
o ponoura
a pena
poni

C'est la toile d'araignée pentrale,
la poile onoure
d'ou-ou la voile,
la plaque anale d'anavou.

(Tu ne lui enlèves rien, dieu,
parce que c'est moi.
Tu ne m'as jamais rien enlevé de cet ordre.
Je l'écris ici pour la première fois,
je le trouve pour la première fois.)

Non la membrane de la voûte,
non le membre omis de ce foutre,
d'une déprédation issu,

mais une carne,
hors membrane,
hors de là où c'est dur ou mou.

Ja passée par le dur et mou,
étendue cette carne en paume,
tirée, tendue comme une paume
                    de main
exsangue de se tenir raide,
noir, violette
de tendre au mou.

Mais quoi donc à la fin, toi, le fou?

It's the penetral* spider veil,
the female onor fur
of either-or the sail,
the anal plate of anayor.

(You lift nothing from it, god,
because it's me.
You never lifted anything of this order from me.
I'm writing it here for the first time,
I'm finding it for the first time.)

Not the membrane of the chasm,
nor the member omitted from this jism,
issued from a depredation,

but an old bag,*
outside membrane,
outside of there where it's hard or soft.

B'now passed through the hard and soft,
spread out this old bag in palm,
pulled, stretched like a palm
                    of hand
bloodless from keeping rigid,
black, violet
from stretching to soft.

But what then in the end, you, the madman?

Moi ?

Cette langue entre quatre gencives,

cette viande entre deux genoux,

ce morceau de trou
pour les fous.

Mais justement pas pour les fous.
Pour les honnêtes,
que rabote un délire à roter partout,

et qui de ce rot
firent la feuille,

écoutez bien:
firent la feuille
du début des générations
dans la carne palmée de mes trous,
à moi.

Lesquels, et de quoi ces trous?

D'âme, d'esprit, de moi, et d'être;
mais à la place où l'on s'en fout,
père, mère, Artaud et itou.

Me?

This tongue between four gums,

this meat between two knees,

this piece of hole
for madmen.

Yet precisely not for madmen.
For respectable men,
whom a delirium to belch everywhere planes,

and who from this belch
made the leaf,

listen closely:
made the leaf
of the beginning of generations
in the palmate old bag of my holes,
mine.

Which holes, holes of what?

Of soul, of spirit, of me, and of being;
but in the place where no one gives a shit,
father, mother, Artaud and artoo.

Dans l'humus de la trame à roues,
dans l'humus soufflant de la trame
de ce vide,
entre dur et mou.

Noir, violet,
raide,
pleutre
et c'est tout.

Ce qui veut dire qu'il y a un os,
où
dieu
s'est mis sur le poète,
pour lui saccager l'ingestion
de ses vers,
tels des pets de tête
qu'il lui soutire par le con,

qu'il lui soutirerait du fond des âges,
jusqu'au fond de son trou de con,

et ce n'est pas un tour de con
qu'il lui joue de cette manière,
c'est le tour de toute la terre
contre qui a des couilles
au con.

Et si on ne comprend pas l'image,
— et c'est ce que je vous entends dire

In the humus of the plot with wheels,
in the breathing humus of the plot
of this void,
between hard and soft.

Black, violet,
rigid,
recreant
and that's all.

Which means that there is a bone,
where
god
sat down on the poet,
in order to sack the ingestion
of his lines,
like the head farts
that he wheedles out of him through his cunt,

that he would wheedle out of him from the bottom of the ages,
down to the bottom of his cunt hole,

and it's not a cunt prank
that he plays on him in this way,
it's the prank of the whole earth
against whoever has balls
in his cunt.

And if you don't get the image,
— and that's what I hear you saying

en rond,
que vous ne comprenez pas l'image
qui est au fond
de mon trou de con, —

c'est que vous ignorez le fond,
non pas des choses,
mais de mon con
à moi,
bien que depuis le fond des âges
vous y clapotiez tous en rond
comme on clabaude un aliénage,
complote à mort une incarcération.

**ge re ghi
regheghi
geghena
e reghena
a gegha
riri**

Entre le cu et la chemise,
entre le foutre et l'infra-mise,
entre le membre et le faux bond,
entre la membrane et la lame,
entre la latte et le plafond,
entre le sperme et l'explosion,
tre l'arête et tre le limon,

in a circle,
that you don't get the image
which is at the bottom
of my cunt hole, —

it's because you don't know the bottom,
not of things,
but of my cunt,
mine,
although since the bottom of the ages
you've all been lapping there in a circle
as if badmouthing an alienage,*
plotting an incarceration to death.

>ge re ghi
>regheghi
>geghena
>e reghena
>a gegha
>riri

Between the ass and the shirt,
between the gism and the under-bet,
between the member and the let down,
between the membrane and the blade,
between the slat and the ceiling,
between the sperm and the explosion,
'tween the fishbone and 'tween the slime,

entre le cu et la main mise
                    de tous
sur la trappe à haute pression
d'un râle d'éjaculation
n'est pas un point
ni une pierre

éclatée morte au pied d'un bond

ni le membre coupé d'une âme
(l'âme n'est plus qu'un vieux dicton)
mais l'atterrante suspension
d'un souffle d'aliénation

violé, tondu, pompé à fond
par toute l'insolente racaille
de tous les empafrés d'étrons
qui n'eurent pas d'autre boustifaille
                    pour vivre
                    que de bouffer
                    Artaud
                    mômo
                    là, où l'on peut piner plus tôt
                    que moi
                    et l'autre bander plus haut
                    que moi
                    en moi-même
s'il a eu soin de mettre la tête
sur la courbure de cet os

between the ass and everyone's
                seizure
of the high-pressure trap
of an ejaculation death rattle
is neither a point
nor a stone

burst dead at the foot of a bound

nor the severed member of a soul
(the soul is no more than an old saw)
but the terrifying suspension
of a breath of alienation

raped, clipped, completely sucked off
by all the insolent riff-raff
of all the turd-buggered
who had no other grub
                in order to live
                than to gobble
                Artaud
                mômo
                there, where one can fuck sooner
                than me
                and the other get hard higher
                than me
                in myself
if he has taken care to put his head
on the curvature of that bone

situé entre anus et sexe,

de cet os sarclé que je dis

dans la crasse
d'un paradis
dont le premier dupé sur terre
ne fut pas le père ou la mère
qui dans cet antre te refit
                    mais
                    JE
vissé dans ma folie.

Et qu'est-ce qui me prit
d'y rouler moi aussi ma vie?
                    MOI,
                    RIEN, *rien.*
Parce que moi,
                    j'y suis,
                    j'y suis
et c'est la vie
qui y roule sa paume obscène.

                    Bien.
                    Et après?

                    Après? Après?
                    Le vieil Artaud
                    est enterré

located between anus and sex,

        of that hoed bone that I say

in the filth
of a paradise
whose first dupe on earth
was not father nor mother
who diddled you in this den
        but
        I
screwed into my madness.

And what seized hold of me
that I too rolled my life there?
        ME,
        NOTHING, *nothing.*
Because I,
        I am there,
        I'm there
and it is life
that rolls its obscene palm there.

        Ok.
        And afterward?

        Afterward? Afterward?
        The old Artaud
        is buried

dans le trou de la cheminée
qu'il tient de sa gencive froide
de ce jour où il fut tué!

        Et après?
        Après?
        Après!
Il est ce trou sans cadre
que la vie voulut encadrer.
Parce qu'il n'est pas un trou
        mais un nez
qui sut toujours trop bien renifler
le vent de l'apocalyptique
        tête
qu'on pompe sur son cu serré,
et que le cu d'Artaud est bon
pour les souteneurs en miserere.

Et toi aussi tu as la gencive,
la gencive droite enterrée,
        dieu,

toi aussi ta gencive est froide
depuis infiniment d'années
que tu m'envoyas ton cu inné
pour voir si j'allais être né
        à la fin
depuis le temps que tu m'espérais

in the chimney hole
he owes to his cold gum
to the day when he was killed!

And afterward?
Afterward?
Afterward!
He is this unframed hole
that life wanted to frame.
Because he is not a hole
but a nose
that always knew all too well to sniff
the wind of the apocalyptic
head
which they suck on his clenched ass,
and that Artaud's ass is good
for pimps in Miserere.

And you too you have your gum,
your right gum buried,
god,

you too your gum is cold
for an infinity of years
since you sent me your innate ass
to see if I was going to be born
at last
since the time you were waiting for me

en raclant
mon ventre d'absent.

menendi anenbi
embenda
tarch inemptle
o marchti rombi
tarch paiolt
a tinemptle
orch pendui
o patendi
a merchit
orch torpch
ta urchpt orchpt
ta tro taurch
campli
ko ti aunch
a ti aunch
aungbli

while scraping
my absentee belly.

menendi anenbi
embenda
tarch inemptle
o marchti rombi
tarch paiolt
a tinemptle
orch pendui
o patendi
a merchit
orch torpch
ta urchpt orchpt
ta tro taurch
campli
ko ti aunch
a ti aunch
aungbli

CENTRE-MÈRE ET PATRON-MINET

Je parle le totem muré

car le totem mural est tel
que les formations visqueuses
de l'être
ne peuvent plus l'enfourcher de près.

C'est sexe carne
ce totem refoulé,

c'est une viande
de répulsion abstruse
ce squelette
qu'on ne peut
mâtiner,

ni de mère, ni
de père inné,

n'étant pas
la viande minette

CENTER-MOTHER AND BOSS-PUSSY

I talk the enwalled totem

for the wall totem is such
that the viscous formations
of being
can no longer straddle it up close

It's old bag sex
this repressed totem,

it's a meat
of abstruse repulsion
this skeleton
that we can't
crossbreed,

neither with mother, nor
with innate father,

not being
the pussy meat

qu'on copule
à patron-minet.

Or la panse
n'était pas affrétée
quand totem
entra dans l'histoire
pour en décourager
                l'entrée.

Et il fallut ventre à ventre cogner
chaque mère qui voulait pénétrer

chatte-mite en patron-minet

dans l'exsangue tube insurgé

comme au centre
de la panacée:

chatte-mite et patron-minet
sont les deux vocables salauds
que père et mère ont
                inventés

pour jouir de lui au plus gros.

Qui ça, lui?

that we copulize*
at peep o'day.

Now the paunch
was not freighted
when totem
entered history
in order to discourage
            the entering.

And it was crucial belly to belly to bang
each mother who wanted to penetrate

pussy-toady* **on boss-pussy**

into the insurgent exsanguine tube

as at the center
of the panacea:

pussy-toady and boss-pussy
are the two sluttish vocables
that father and mother
            invented

to get the crudest pleasure out of him.

Who that, him?

Totem étranglé,

comme un membre dans une poche
que la vie *froche*
                    de si près,

qu'à la fin le totem muré
crèvera le ventre de naître

à travers la piscine enflée
du sexe de la mère ouverte

par la clef de **patron-minet.**

Strangled totem,

like a member in a pocket
that life *frockets**
            so close,

that in the end the enwalled totem
will burst the belly of birthing

through the swollen piscina
of the mother's sex organ opened

by **boss-pussy's** key.

INSULTE À L'INCONDITIONNÉ

C'est par la barbaque,
la sale barbaque
que l'on exprime

                le,

qu'on ne sait pas

                que

                se placer hors

                pour être sans,

                avec, ——

la barbaque
bien crottée et mirée
dans le cu d'une poule
morte et désirée.

Insult To The Unconditioned

It's through third-rate meat,
dirty third-rate meat
that we express

the,

that we do not know

that

placing ourselves outside

so as to be without,

with, —

third-rate meat
really befouled and mirrored
in the ass of a tart
dead and desired.

Désirée, dis-je,
mais sans juter
des esquilles
blanches, lapées,

      (mornes de morve
      la salive)

      la salive
      de son dentier.

Avec la barbaque
qu'on se débarrasse
des **rats** de **l'inconditionné.**

Qui n'ont jamais senti
      que

      la non-forme,

      le hors-lieu
de la rogne sans condition,
appelée *le sans-condition,*

l'interférence de l'action,

le transfert par déportation;

le rétablissement hors coupure,

Desired, say I,
but without juicing off
white, lapped up
bone splinters,

> (buttes of mucous
> the saliva)

> the saliva
> from her false teeth.

With third-rate meat
let's get rid of
the **rats** of **the unconditioned.**

> Who have never felt
> that

> the non-form

> the outside-place
of the foul temper without condition
called *the without-condition,*

the interference of action,

the transfer by deportation;

the reestablishment outside incision,

la coupure des colmatations;

l'assise enfin
dans le non-hors,

l'imposition du dehors qui dort,
comme un dedans, éclaté des latrines
du canal où l'on chie la mort,

ne valent pas les desquamations
du con d'une moniche morte

quand la boniche qui le porte
pisse en arc-boutant
son pis

pour traverser
la syphilis.

the cutting of clogations;*

in short the foundation
in the non-outside,

the imposition of the outside which sleeps,
like an inside, burst from the latrines
of the canal where we shit death,

are not worth the desquamations
from the cunt of a dead tench*

when the wench who bears it
pisses while buttressing
her tit

in order to cross
syphilis.

L'EXÉCRATION DU PÈRE-MÈRE

L'intelligence est venue après la sottise,
laquelle l'a toujours sodomisée de près, —
ET APRÈS.

Ce qui donne une idée de l'infini trajet.

EXECRATION OF THE FATHER-MOTHER

Intelligence came after stupidity,
which had always sodomized it closely, —
AND THEN.

Which gives an idea of the infinite journey.

D'une préméditation de non-être,
d'une criminelle incitation de peut-être
est venue la réalité,
comme du hasard qui la forniquait.

From a premeditation of non-being,
from a criminal incitement of may-be
came reality,
as from chance which was fornicating it.

Je te condamne parce que tu sais pourquoi. . . je te condamne, —

et moi, je ne le sais pas.

I condemn you because you know why. . . I condemn you, —

and me, I don't know why.

Ce n'est pas un esprit qui a fait les choses,

It is not a spirit which has made things,

mais un corps, lequel pour être avait besoin de crapuler,
avec sa verge à bonder son nez.

klaver striva
cavour tavina
scaver kavina
okar triva

but a body, which in order to be needed to wallow in vice,
with its penis for cramming its nose.

        klaver striva
        cavour tavina
        scaver kavina
        okar triva

Pas de philosophie, pas de question, pas d'être,
pas de néant, pas de refus, pas de peut-être,

et pour le reste

crotter, crotter;

**ÔTER LA CROÛTE
DU PAIN BROUTÉ;**

No philosophy, no question, no being,
no nothingness, no refusal, no may-be,

as for the rest

to crap, to crap;

STRIP THE CRUST
FROM THE BROWSED BREAD;

ignobles déprédations
d'avinés dans les ciboires et les psautiers,
le vin des messes,
les crécelles des bonzes tartriques,
sortis innés d'un mamtram faussé,
tartre encroûtée d'un ancien crime,
latrines de sublimité!

l'heure approche où le puisatier qu'on déféqua dans les poubelles
    baptismales des bénitiers,
se rendra compte qu'il était moi.

ignoble depredations
of winos in the ciboria and the psalters,
the wine of the Masses,
the rattles of tartaric bonzes,
emerged innate from a warped mamtram,[*]
encrusted tartar of an ancient crime,
latrines of sublimity!

the hour draws near when the well driller who was defecated into
    the baptismal garbage cans of holy water basins,
will realize that he was me.

Or, je le sais.

Now, I know this.

Et ce fut toujours vidange pour ange,

And it was always drainage for angels,

et ma vidange passa la leur,
le jour où
forcé de sarcler dans les gommes syphilisées
d'une crasse depuis toujours constituée,
je compris que le sarclé c'était moi, —
et que vous défèque ce qu'on a déféqué,
si l'on ne prend pas
très à l'avance
la précaution de syphiliser,

la verge abcès
DANS LA RENIFLE DU MUFLE DE LA VOLONTÉ.

and my drainage surpassed theirs,
the day when
forced to hoe in the syphilitic resins
of a filth organized from the very beginning,
I understood that what was hoed was me, —
and that you defecate what they have defecated,
if they do not take
well in advance
the precaution to syphilize,

the penis abscess
IN THE SNIFF OF THE MUZZLE OF THE WILL.

Et que le plat s'allume en volume,

car le plat n'a pas de volume,
et c'est le volume qui est le plat;

le volume mange le plat
qui tourne de tous côtés pour ça.

And let flatness light up in volume,

for the flat has no volume,
and it is the volume which is the flat;

the volume eats the flat,
which turns on all sides because of that.

La breloque interne
était que
le partant qui est
toujours là

ne peut
bien se supporter
là

que
parce que
l'immobile
le porte

en fondant
toujours,

le portant qui est
de toujours,

qu'il emporte

depuis toujours.

The internal watch charm
was that
the departer who is
always there

can
bear being
there

only
because
the unmoved
bears him

by always
melting

the bearer who
always is,

who it has been bearing away

from the very beginning.

Les esprits se procurent une minute d'intelligence
en me plongeant, moi, dans un bas-fond
qu'ils se procurent
par absence de nourriture ou d'opium
dans mon bedon,
maelström sur maelström de fond (de culture de par le fond),

après quoi ils retournent à leur ancestrale putréfaction.

Spirits procure for themselves an instant of intelligence
by plunging me, me, into a lower depth
which they procure for themselves
through the absence of nourishment or opium
in my potbelly,
maelstrom upon maelstrom of depth (of culture by way of the bottom),

after which they return to their ancestral putrefaction.

Si je me réveille tous les matins avec autour de moi
cette épouvantable odeur de foutre,
ce n'est pas que j'ai été succubé par les esprits de
l'au-delà, —

mais que les hommes de ce monde-ci
se passent le mot dans leur «perisprit»:

frottement de leurs couilles pleines,
sur le canal de leur anus
bien caressé et bien saisi,
afin de me pomper la vie.

If I wake up every morning surrounded by
this appalling odor of jism,
it is not because I have been succubused by the spirits of
the beyond, —

but because the men of this world here
pass the word around in their "perisprit":*

rubbing of their full balls,
along the canal of their anus
nicely caressed and nicely grasped,
in order to pump out my life.

«C'est que votre sperme est très bon,
m'a dit un jour
un flic du Dôme
qui se posait en connaisseur,
et quand on est «si bon»,
«si bon», dame,
on surpaye
son renom.»

Car probablement il en sortait
de ce sperme, si bon,
si bon;
et il l'avait baratté et sucé
à l'instar de
toute la terre,
tout le long de la nuit passée.

"It's that your sperm is very good,
a cop from the Dôme
said to me one day
who set himself up as a connoisseur,
and when one is 'so good,'
'so good,' by god
one pays too much
for fame."

For probably he emerged from it
from this sperm, so good,
so good;
and he had churned and sucked it
like everyone
else in the world
the whole last night.

Et je sentis son âme virer,
ET JE LE VIS VERDIR DES PAUPIÈRES,
passer du copinage à la peur,

car il sentit que j'allais cogner.

And I saw his soul veer,
AND I SAW HIS EYELIDS TURN VERDIGRIS,
passing from chumminess to fear,

.   for he felt that I was going to strike.

Pas de tutoiement, ni de copinage,
jamais avec moi,
pas plus dans la vie que dans la pensée.

Et je ne sais pas si ce n'est pas en rêve que j'entendis la fin de sa phrase:
«et quand on est si bon, si bon, dame, on surpaye son renom.»

No first name basis, nor chumminess,
never with me,
no more in life than in thought.

And I don't know if it isn't in a dream that I heard the end of his
    phrase:
"and when one is so good, so good, by god, one pays too much for
    fame."

Drôle de rêve où le squelette
de l'église et de la police
se tutoyaient
dans l'*arsenic* de ma liqueur séminale.

Car la vieille complainte revenait
de l'histoire du vieil Artaud assassiné
dans l'autre vie,
et qui n'entrera plus dans celle-ci.

Mais est-ce que je n'y suis pas entré
dans cette foutue branleuse vie
depuis cinquante ans que je suis né.

Weird dream where the skeleton
of the church and the police
were on a first name basis
in the *arsenic* of my seminal liquor.

For the old lament was coming back
from the story of the old Artaud assassinated
in the other life,
and who will not again enter this one.

But haven't I entered it
entered this fucked-up jerk-off life
in the fifty years since I've been born.

P.-S.—C'est une complainte que l'on récitait il n'y a pas encore six siècles dans les lycées de l'Afghanistan où Artaud s'orthographiait arto: *a.r.t.o. La même complainte se retrouve dans les vieilles légendes mazdéennes ou étrusques et dans des passages du Popol-Vuh.*

P.S. — It's a lament that was recited not quite six centuries ago in the high schools of Afganistan where Artaud was spelled arto: *a.r.t.o.*
The same lament is found in old Mazdean or Etruscan legends and in passages of the Popol Vuh.

ALIÉNATION ET MAGIE NOIRE

Les asiles d'aliénés sont des réceptacles de magie noire conscients et
    prémédités,

et ce n'est pas seulement que les médecins favorisent la magie par leurs
    thérapeutiques intempestives et hybrides,
c'est qu'ils en font.

S'il n'y avait pas eu de médecins
il n'y aurait jamais eu de malades,
pas de squelettes de morts
malades à charcuter et dépiauter,
car c'est par les médecins et non par les malades que la société a com-
    mencé.

Ceux qui vivent, vivent des morts.
Et il faut aussi que la mort vive;
et il n'y a rien comme un asile d'aliénés pour couver doucement la mort,
    et tenir en couveuse des morts.

Cela a commencé 4000 ans avant Jésus-christ cette thérapeutique de la
    mort lente,

ALIENATION AND BLACK MAGIC

Insane asylums are conscious and premeditated receptacles of black
    magic,

and it is not only that doctors encourage magic with their inopportune
    and hybrid therapies,
it is how they use it.

If there had been no doctors
there would never have been patients,
no skeletons of the diseased
dead to butcher and flay,
for it is through doctors and not through patients that society began.

Those who live, live off the dead.
And it is likewise necessary that death live;
and there is nothing like an insane asylum for gently incubating death,
    and for keeping the dead in incubators.

It began 4000 years before Jesus christ this therapy of slow death,

et la médecine moderne, complice en cela de la plus sinistre et crapuleuse magie, passe ses morts à l'électro-choc ou à l'insulinothérapie afin de bien chaque jour vider ses haras d'hommes de leur moi,

et de les présenter ainsi vides,

ainsi fantastiquement

disponibles et vides,

aux obscènes sollicitations anatomiques et atomiques

de l'état appelé **Bardo,** livraison du **barda** de vivre aux exigences du non-moi.

Le Bardo est l'affre de mort dans lequel le moi tombe en flaque,

et il y a dans l'électro-choc un état flaque

par lequel passe tout traumatisé,

et qui lui donne, non plus à cet instant de connaître, mais d'affreusement et désespérément méconnaître ce qu'il fut, quand il était soi, quoi, loi, moi, roi, toi, zut et CA.

J'y suis passé et ne l'oublierai pas.

La magie de l'électro-choc draine un râle, elle plonge le commotionné dans ce râle par lequel on quitte la vie.

Or, les électro-chocs du Bardo ne furent jamais une expérience, et râler dans l'électro-choc du Bardo, comme dans le Bardo de l'électro-choc, c'est déchiqueter une expérience sucée par les larves du non-moi, et que l'homme ne retrouvera pas.

Au milieu de cette palpitation et de cette respiration de tous les autres

and modern medicine, an accomplice in this of the most sinister and
  crapulous magic, subjects its dead to electroshock or to insulin ther-
  apy so as daily to throughly empty its stud farms of men of their
  egos,
and to expose them thus empty,
thus fantastically
available and empty,
to the obscene anatomical and atomic solicitations
of the state called **Bardo,** delivery of the **full kit** for living to the
  demands of the non-ego.

Bardo is the death throes in which the ego falls in a puddle,
and there is in electroshock a puddle state
through which everyone traumatized passes,
and which causes him, no longer at this moment to know, but to dread-
  fully and desperately misjudge what he was, when* he was himself,
  his own elf, his fief, wife, life, tripe, damnit and THAT.

I went through it and I won't forget it.

The magic of electroshock drains a death rattle, it plunges the shocked
  into that rattle with which we leave life.

But, the electroshocks of Bardo were never an experiment, and to death
  rattle in the electroshock of Bardo, as in the Bardo of electroshock,
  is to mangle an experiment sucked by the larvae of the non-ego, and
  that man will not recapture.
In the midst of this palpitation and this respiration of all the others who

qui assiègent celui qui, comme disent les Mexicains, raclant pour l'entamer l'écorce de sa râpe, *coule de tous côtés sans loi.*

La médecine soudoyée ment chaque fois qu'elle présente un malade
    guéri par les introspections électriques de sa méthode,
je n'ai vu, moi, que des terrorisés de la méthode,
incapables de retrouver leur moi.

Qui a passé par l'électro-choc du Bardo, et le Bardo de l'électro-choc,
    ne remonte plus jamais de ses ténèbres, et la vie a baissé d'un
    cran.
J'y ai connu ces moléculations souffle après souffle du râle des authen-
    tiques agonisants.

Ce que les Tarahumaras du Mexique appellent le crachat de la râpe,
    l'escarbille du charbon sans dents.

Perte d'un pan de l'euphorie première qu'on eut un jour à se sentir
    vivant, déglutinant et mastiquant.

C'est ainsi que l'électro-choc comme le Bardo crée des larves, il fait de
    tous les états pulvérisés du patient, de tous les faits de son passé des
    larves inutilisables pour le présent et qui ne cessent plus d'assiéger
    le présent.

Or, je le répète, le Bardo c'est la mort, et **la mort n'est qu'un état de
magie noire qui n'existait pas il n'y a pas si longtemps.**

besiege the one who, as the Mexicans say, scraping to broach the
bark with his grater, *flows lawlessly from all sides.*

Bribed medicine lies each time that it presents a patient cured by the
electrical introspections of its method,
as for me, I've seen only those who have been terrorized by the method,
incapable of recovering their egos.

Who has gone through the electroshock of Bardo, and the Bardo of
electroshock, never climbs up again from its tenebrae, and life has
slipped a notch.
I've known there these moleculations breath upon breath of the death
rattle of authentically agonizing people.

What the Tarahumaras of Mexico call the spittle of the grater, the cin-
der of toothless coal.

Loss of a slap of the first euphoria that you had one day feeling yourself
alive, swallowing* and chewing.

It is thus that electroshock like Bardo creates larvae, it turns all the
patient's pulverized states, all the facts of his past into larvae which
are unusable in the present yet which never cease beseiging the pre-
sent.

Now, I repeat, Bardo is death, and **death is only a state of black magic
which did not exist not so long ago.**

Créer ainsi artificiellement la mort comme la médecine actuelle l'entreprend c'est favoriser un reflux du néant qui n'a jamais profité à personne,
mais dont certains profiteurs prédestinés de l'homme se repaissent depuis longtemps.

En fait, depuis un certain point du temps.

Lequel?

Celui où il fallut choisir entre renoncer à être homme ou devenir un aliéné évident.

Mais quelle garantie les aliénés évidents de ce monde ont-ils d'être soignés par d'authentiques vivants?

farfadi
ta azor
tau ela
auela
a
tara
ila

FIN

To thus create death artificially as present-day medicine attempts to do
is to encourage a reflux of the nothingness which has never been to
anyone's benefit,
but off which certain predestined human profiteers have been eating
their fill for a long time.

Actually, since a certain point in time.

Which one?

That point when it was necessary to choose between renouncing being
a man and becoming an obvious madman.

But what guarantee do the obvious madmen of this world have of being
nursed by the authentically living?

> **farfadi**
> **ta azor**
> **tau ela**
> **auela**
> **a**
> **tara**
> **ila**

THE END

Une page blanche pour séparer le texte du livre qui est fini de tout le grouillement du Bardo qui apparaît dans les limbes de l'électro-choc.

Et dans ces limbes une typographie spéciale, laquelle est là pour abjecter dieu, mettre en retrait les paroles verbales auxquelles une valeur spéciale a voulu être attribuée.

ANTONIN ARTAUD.
12 janvier 1948.

A blank page to separate the text of the book, which is finished from all
the swarming of Bardo which appeared in the limbo of elec-
troshock.

And in this limbo a special typography, which is there to abject god, to
background the verbal words to which one wanted to attribute a
special value.

ANTONIN ARTAUD

12 January 1948

ARTAUD LE MÔMO

ARTAUD THE MÔMO

tu t'en vas,
dit l'immonde tutoiement du Bardo,
et tu es toujours là,

you're leaving, kid,
says the scummy familiarity of Bardo,
and you're still there,

tu n'es plus là
mais rien ne te quitte,
tu as tout conservé
sauf toi-même
et que t'importe puisque
le monde
est là.

Le -
monde,
mais ce n'est plus moi.
Et que t'importe,
dit le Bardo,
          c'est moi.

you're no longer there
but nothing leaves you,
you've kept everything
except yourself
and what's it to you since
the world
is there.

The
world,
but it's no longer me.
And what's it to you, kid,
says Bardo,
it's me.

P.S. — J'ai à me plaindre d'avoir dans l'électro-choc rencontré des morts
que je n'aurais pas voulu voir.

Les mêmes,
que ce livre imbécile appelé
                    Bardo Todol
draine et propose depuis un peu plus de quatre mille ans.

Pourquoi?

Je demande simplement:
Pourquoi?...

P.S. — I want to complain about having met in electroshock dead peo-
ple whom I wouldn't have chosen to see.

The same ones,
whom this imbecilic book called
                    Bardo Todol
has been draining and proposing for a little more than four thousand
years.

Why?

I simply ask:
Why?...

LA CULTURE INDIENNE

INDIAN CULTURE

Je suis venu au Mexique prendre contact avec la Terre Rouge
et elle pue comme elle embaume;
elle sent bon comme elle puait.

Cafre d'urine de la pente d'un vagin dur,
et qui se refuse quand on le prend.

Camphre urinaire de l'éminence d'un vagin mort,
et qui vous soufflette quand on l'étend,

quand on mire du haut du Mirador du Pitre,
tombe cloutée du père affreux,

le trou à creux, l'âcre trou creux, où bout le cycle des poux rouges,
cycle des poux solaires rouges,
tout blancs dans le lacis des veines de l'un deux.

Qui ça deux, et lequel des deux?
Qui, les deux?
au temps
septante fois maudit
où l'homme
                    se croisant lui-même
naissait fils

I came to Mexico to make contact with the Red Earth
and it stinks the same way that it embalms;
it smells good the same way that it stank.

Kaffir of urine from the slope of a tough vagina,
which when we grab it refuses to give.

Urinary camphor from the bulge of a dead vagina,
which smacks us when we spread it out,

when we eye, from the height of the Clown's Mirador,
the ghastly father's hobnailed tomb,

the hollowed hole, acrid hollow hole, where the cycle of red lice boils,
cycle of solar red lice,
all white in the veiny network of the one two.

Who that two, and which one of the two?
Who, the two?
in the age
seventy times cursed
when man
                crossing himself
was being born son

de sa sodomie
sur son propre cu
endurci.
Pourquoi deux d'eux,
et pourquoi de DEUX?

Pitre affreux de père mimire,
immonde pitri parasite, dans creux mamiche retiré du feu!

Car les soleils qui passent tout ronds
ne sont rien auprès du pied bot,
de l'immense articulation
de la vieille jambe gangrène,
vieille jambe ossuaire gangrène,
où mûrit un bouclier d'os,

la levée souterraine, guerrière,
des boucliers de tous les os.

Qu'est-ce à dire?

Ça veut dire que papa-mama n'encule plus le pédéraste inné,
l'immonde boutis des partouses chrétiennes,
interlope entre ji et cri,
contracté en
                    jiji-cricri,

et ça veut dire que la guerre
remplacera le père-mère

of his sodomy
on his own callused
butt.
Why two of them,
and why of TWO?

Ghastly clown of the pusseying father,*
filthy parasitic clone, in the hollow mamuffin* pulled out of the fire!

For the suns swallowed whole
are nothing compared to the clubfoot,
of the immense articulation
of old leg gangrene,
old boneyard leg gangrene,
where a shield of bones is ripening,

the warlike, underground uprising
of the shields of all the bones.

What does it mean?

It means that daddy-mommy* no longer buggers the innate pederast,
the filthy tusk holes* of Christian fuckfests,
interloper between ji and cry,
contracted in
               jiji-crycry,

and it means that war
will replace the father-mother

là où le cu faisait barrière
contre la peste nourricière
de la Terre Rouge enterrée
sous le cadavre du guerrier
                    mort
pour n'avoir pas voulu passer
par le périple du serpent
qui se mord la queue par devant
cependant que papa-maman
lui mettent le derrière en sang.

Et qu'à y regarder de près,
dans la tranche tuméfiée de la jambe,
du vieux fémur couperosé
tombent
                    ça pue
                    et ça puait;
et resurgit le vieux guerrier
de la cruauté insurgée,
de l'indicible cruauté
de vivre et de n'avoir pas d'être
qui puisse vous justifier;
et tombent
dans le trou ancré
de la terre vue de haut, et en perce,
tous les bouts de langue éclairés,
et qui un jour se crurent âmes,
n'étant même pas des volontés;

there where the butt raised a barrier
against the foster plague
of the Red Earth buried
under the corpse of the warrior
                    dead
for having refused to pass
through the periplus of the serpent
biting its tail from in front
while daddy-mommy
make his buttocks bloody.

And if scrutinizing closely,
in the tumified slice of leg,
from the old blotched thighbone
there fall
                    it stinks
                    and it stank;
and there resurges the old warrior
of insurgent cruelty,
of the unspeakable cruelty
of living and not having a being
who could justify you;
and there fall
into the anchored hole
of the earth seen from above, and abroach,
all the tips of lit-up tongue,
and which one day believed themselves souls,
not even being wills;

montent
tous les éclairs
de la schlague de ma main morte,
contre la langue soulevée,

et les sexes de volonté,

qui sont à peine des mots jetés,
lesquels n'ont pas pu prendre d'être;

mais tombent mieux que des soleils
rejetés,
dans la cave où s'entretuaient
papa-maman
et pédéraste,
le fils d'avant que ça puait.

Quand l'âne solaire se croyait bon!

Et où était le ciel dans son rond?

Où l'on était,
            dehors,
tout con
de sentir le ciel
            dans son con,

sans rien qui pût faire barrière contre le vide,
où

INDIAN CULTURE

there rise
all the lightnings
from the flogging of my dead hand,
against the tongue in revolt,

and the sexes of will,

which are barely flung words,
that could not snag being;

but fall better than rejected
suns
into the cellar where, killing each other,
were daddy-mommy
and pederast,
the son from before it stank.

When the solar donkey believed himself good!

And where was the sky in its round?

Where one was,
                outside,
completely cunt
from feeling the sky
                in his cunt,

without anything that could raise a barrier against the void,
where

pas de fond
et pas d'aplomb,
et pas de face,
ni de haut,
et où tout vous rapplique au fond,
quand on est droit tout de son long.

no bottom
and no upright
and no face,
nor top,
and where all hustles back to you at the bottom,
when one is all his length straight.

CI-GÎT

HERE LIES

Moi, Antonin Artaud, je suis mon fils, mon père, ma mère,
et moi;
niveleur du périple imbécile où s'enferre l'engendrement
le périple papa-maman
et l'enfant,
suie du cu de la grand-maman,
beaucoup plus que du père-mère.

Ce qui veut dire qu'avant maman et papa
qui n'avaient ni père ni mère,
dit-on,
et où donc les auraient-ils pris,
eux,
quand ils devinrent ce conjoint
unique
que ni l'épouse ni l'époux
n'a pu voir assis ou debout,
avant cet improbable trou
que l'esprit se cherche pour nous,
pour nous
dégoûter un peu plus de nous,
était ce corps inemployable,
fait de viande et de sperme fou,
ce corps pendu, d'avant les poux,

Me, Antonin Artaud, I am my son, my father, my mother,
                    and me;
leveler of the imbecilic periplus where begetting impales itself,
the daddy-mommy periplus
                    and the child,
soot from grandma's ass,
much more than father-mother's.

Which means that before mommy and daddy
who had neither father nor mother,
                    it is said,
and where indeed would they have got them,
                    they,
when they became this unique
                    conjunct
no husband nor wife
could have seen sit or stand,
before this improbable hole
the spirit feels out for us,
                              to fill us
with a little more self-disgust,
was this unemployable body,
made of meat and mad sperm,
this body hanged, from before lice,

suant sur l'impossible table
du ciel
son odeur calleuse d'atome,
sa rogomeuse odeur d'abject
détritus
éjecté du somme
de l'Inca mutilé des doigts

qui pour idée avait un bras
mais n'avait de main qu'une paume
morte, d'avoir perdu ses doigts
à force de tuer de rois.

.

sweating on the impossible table
of heaven
its callous atom odor,
its croupous odor of abject
detritus
ejected from the snooze
of the finger-mutilated Inca

who for an idea had an arm
but had as a hand only a dead
palm, having lost his fingers
by dint of killing kings.

Avant donc DIZJE tout cela,
était la radineuse,
était cette râleuse

cause du ventre
au ciel bouffant

et qui chemina,
la hideuse,
7 fois 7 ans,
7 trilliards d'ans,
suivant la piteuse
arithmétique
de l'antique goémantie,

jusqu'à ce que des mamelles en sang
éjectées
de la cendre creuse
qui suinte du firmament
lui jaillît enfin cet enfant
maudit de l'homme
et de l'enfer même,

mais que dieu
plus laid que Satan

Hence SEZ-I before all that,
was the stingy old bag,
this grouchy nag

cause of the belly
with its bouffant heaven

who trudged along
— the hideous hag —
7 times 7 years,
7 trilliard years,
following the piteous
arithmetic
of ancient geomancy,

until from blood-smeared breasts
ejected
from the hollow ash
seeping from the firmament
spurted forth at last this child
cursed by man
and by hell itself,

but whom god
uglier than Satan

élut pour faire
la pige à l'homme

et il l'appela être
cet enfant
qui avait un sexe
entre ses dents.

Car un autre enfant
était vrai,
était réel,

sans grand-maman
qui pût l'élire
de tout son ventre,

de toute sa fesse
de chien puant,

sorti seul
de la main en sang
de l'Inca mutilé des doigts.

elected to take
the shine out of man

and he called him being
this child
who had a sex organ
between his teeth.

For another child
was true,
was real,

with no grandma
who could elect him
with her whole belly,

with her whole buttock
of a stinking dog,

emerged alone
from the finger-mutilated Inca's
blood-smeared hand.

Ici faisant marcher les cymbales de fer
je prends la basse route à gouges
dans l'œsophage de l'œil droit

sous la tombe du plexus roide
qui sur la route fait un coude
pour dégager l'enfant de droit.

> **nuyon kidi**
> **nuyon kadan**
> **nuyon kada**
> **tara dada i i**
> **ota papa**
> **ota strakman**
> **tarma strapido**
> **ota rapido**
> **ota brutan**
> **otargugido**
> **ote krutan**

Car je fus Inca mais pas roi.

Here working the iron cymbals
I take the low road of gouges
in the esophagus of the right eye

under the tomb of the rigid plexus
which on the road sharply flexes
to extricate the child by right.

> **nuyon kidi**
> **nuyon kadan**
> **nuyon kada**
> **tara dada i i**
> **ota papa**
> **ota strakman**
> **tarma strapido**
> **ota rapido**
> **ota brutan**
> **otargugido**
> **ote krutan**

For I was Inca but not king.

kilzi
trakilzi
faildor
bara bama
baraba
mince

etretili

TILI

te pince

dans la *falzourchte*
de tout or,
dans la déroute
de tout corps.

Et il n'y avait ni soleil ni personne,
pas un être en avant de moi,
non, pas d'être qui me tutoyât.

Je n'avais que quelques fidèles qui ne cessaient de mourir pour moi.

Quand ils furent trop morts pour vivre,
je ne vis plus que des haineux,
les mêmes qui guignaient leur place,
en combattant à côté d'eux,
trop lâches pour lutter contre eux.

Mais qui les avait vus?

kilzi
trakilzi
faildor
bara bama
baraba
mince

etretili
TILI
tweeks you
in the *pantabazooms**
of all gold,
in the rout
of all body.

And there was no sun, no one,
not a single being ahead of me,
no, no being on a first name basis with me.

I had only a few faithful who didn't cease dying for me.

When they were too dead to live,
I saw only the hateful,
the same who coveted their place,
while battling beside them,
too cowardly to struggle against them.

But who had seen them?

Personne.

Myrmidons de la Perséphone
                    Infernale,
microbes de tout geste en creux,
glaires pitreux d'une loi morte,
kystes de qui se viole entre eux,
langues de l'avaricieux
forceps
gratté sur son urine
                    même,
latrines de la morte osseuse,
que taraude toujours la même
vigueur
                    morne,
du même feu,

                    dont l'antre
innovateur d'un nœud
                    terrible,

mis en clôture
de vie mère,

est la vipère
de mes œufs.

No one.

Myrmidons of the Infernal
                    Persephone,
microbes of each concave gesture,
buffoonic phlegm of a dead law,
cysts of who rapes herself among them,
tongues of the avaricious
forceps
scraped on her urine
                    itself,
latrines of the bony dead woman,
always screw-cut with the same
bleak
                    vigor,
of the same fire,

                    whose lair
innovator of a terrible
                    knot,

encloistered
with mother life,

is the viper (father life)*
of my eggs.

Car c'est la fin qui est le commencement.
Et cette fin
est celle-même
qui élimine
tous les moyens.

For it is the end which is the beginning.
And this end
is the very one
that eliminates
all means.

Et maintenant,
            vous tous, les êtres,
j'ai à vous dire que vous m'avez toujours fait caguer.
            Et allez vous faire
            engruper
            la moumoute
            de la parpougnête,
            morpions
            de l'éternité.

And now,
    all of you, beings,
I have to tell you that you've always made me crap.
   So go get
   the quim-wig
   for your scrubby grope-slope*
   croupswarmed,
   you crab lice
   of eternity.

Je ne me rencontrerai pas une fois de plus avec des êtres qui avalèrent le
    clou de vie.

Et je me rencontrai un jour avec les êtres qui avalèrent le clou de vie,
— sitôt que j'eus perdu ma mamelle matrice,

et l'être me tordit sous lui,
et dieu me reversa à elle.
            (LE SALIGAUD.)

Not once more will I be found with beings who swallowed the nail
    of life.

And one day I found myself with the beings who swallowed the
    nail of life
— as soon as I lost my matrix mamma,

and the being twisted me under him,
and god poured me back to her.
                (THE MOTHERFUCKER)

C'est ainsi que l'on
tira de moi
papa et maman
et la friture de ji en
Cri
au sexe (centre)
du grand étranglement,
d'où fut tiré ce croi
                    sement de la bière
(morte)
et de la matière,
qui donna vie
à Jizo-cri
quand de la fiente de
            moi mort
fut tiré
le sang
dont se dore
            toute vie usurpée
            dehors.

This is how
daddy and mommy were
pulled out of me
and the dish of fried ji in
Cry
at the sex organ (center)
of the great strangling,
from which was pulled this cros
                              seeding of the coffin
(dead)
and of matter
which gave life
to Jizo-cry
when from the guano of
            me dead
was drawn
the blood
with which each life
            usurped outside gilds
            itself.

C'est ainsi que:
le grand secret de la culture indienne
est de ramener le monde à zéro,
toujours,

mais plutôt
        1° trop tard que plus tôt,

        2° ce qui veut dire
           plus tôt
           que trop tôt,

        3° ce qui veut dire que le plus tard ne
           peut revenir que si plus tôt a mangé
           trop tôt,

        4° ce qui veut dire que dans le temps
           le plus tard
           est ce qui précède
           et le trop tôt
           et le plus tôt,

        5° et que si précipité soit plus tôt
           le trop tard

And* that is how:
the great secret of Indian culture
is to lead the world back to zero,
always,

but rather

        1° too late than sooner,

        2° which means
           sooner
           than too soon,

        3° which means that the latest can
           come back only if sooner has eaten
           too soon,

        4° which means that in time
           the latest
           is that which comes before
           and the too soon
           and the sooner,

        5° and that however hurried sooner may be
           even later

qui ne dit pas mot
est toujours là,

qui point par point
désemboîte
tous les plus tôt.

which does not say a word
is always there,

which point by point
disencases
all the sooners.

COMMENTAIRE

Ils vinrent, tous les saligauds,
après le grand désemboîtage,
manifesté de bas en haut.

1° om-let cadran

(ceci chuchoté:)

Vous ne saviez pas ça
que l'état
ŒUF
était l'état
anti-Artaud
par excellence
et que pour empoisonner Artaud
il n'y a rien
de tel que de battre
une bonne omelette
dans les espaces
visant le point
gélatineux

COMMENTARY

They came, all the motherfuckers,
after the great disencasement
manifested from bottom to top.

    1° om-let dial

                  (this whispered:)

    You didn't know this
    that the EGG
              state
    was the anti-
    Artaud state
    par excellence
    and that to poison Artaud
    there is nothing
    like whisking up
    a good omelette
    in the spaces
    aiming at the gelatinous
    point

qu'Artaud
cherchant l'homme à faire
a fui
comme une peste horrible
et c'est ce point
qu'on remet en lui,
rien de tel qu'une bonne omelette
fourrée poison, cyanure, câpres,
transmise par l'air à son cadavre
pour désarticuler Artaud
dans l'anathème de ses os
PENDUS SUR L'INTERNE CADASTRE.

et 2° **palaoulette tirant**
largalalouette te titrant

3° **tuban titi tarftan** de la tête et de la
tête te visant

4° **lomonculus du frontal poince**
et de la pince te putant

il bascule au patron puant,
ce capitaliste arrogant
des limbes
nageant vers le recollement
du père-mère au sexe enfant
afin de vider le corps entière,
entièrement de sa matière

which Artaud
searching for the man to be made
has fled
like a horrible plague
and it is this point
they put back in him,
nothing like a good poison
cyanide and capers stuffed omelette,
transmitted by the air to his cadaver
to disarticulate Artaud
in the anathema of his bones
HANGED ON THE INTERNAL CADASTRE.

and 2° **nolarking* extricating
lotsamalarkey titrating you**

3° **tuban titi tarftan** of the head and from
the head targeting you

4° **lomunculous of the frontal punc
and of the forceps whoring you**

he teeters to the stinking boss,
this arrogant capitalist
of limbo
swimming toward the regluing
of father-mother to the child sex organ
in order to drain the body entire,
entirely of its matter

et d'y mettre à la place, qui?
Celui que l'être et le néant
fit,
comme l'on donne à faire pipi.

222

and to put in its place, who?
The one whom being and nothingness
made,
as one gives to make peepee.

ET ILS, ONT TOUS FOUTU LE CAMP.

HERE LIES

AND THEY, ALL GOT THE FUCK OUT.

Non, il reste la vrille affreuse,
la vrille-crime,
cette affreuse,
vieux clou, gendron,
déviation au profit du gendre faux
de la douleur sciée de l'os,

Ne voit-on pas que le gendre faux,
c'est Jizi-cri,
déjà connu au Mexique
bien avant sa fuite à Jérusalem sur un âne,
et le crucifiement d'Artaud au Golgotha.
Artaud
qui savait qu'il n'y a pas d'esprit
mais un corps
qui se refait comme l'engrenage du cadavre à dents,
dans la gangrène
                    du fémur
                    dedans.

HERE LIES

No, there remains the ghastly gimlet,
the gimlet-crime,
this dreadful,
old nail, stud-in-law,*
deviation profiting the fake son-in-law
of the pain sawed from the bone,

Don't we see that the fake son-in-law,
it's Jizi-cry,
already known in Mexico
long before his flight to Jerusalem on an ass,
and the crucifying of Artaud at Golgotha.
Artaud
who knew that there was no spirit
but a body
that repairs itself like the gearing of a toothed cadaver,
in the gangrene
                    of the thighbone
                    within.

dakantala
dakis tekel
ta redaba
ta redabel
de stra muntils
o ept anis
o ept atra

de la douleur

suée

dans

l'os. —

Tout vrai langage
est incompréhensible,
comme la claque
du claque-dents;
ou le claque (bordel)
du fémur à dents (en sang).

dakantala
dakis tekel
ta redaba
ta redabel
de stra muntils
o ept anis
o ept atra

of the pain

        sweated

in

        the bone. —

All true language
is incomprehensible,
like the clap
of clapperdudgeons;
or the claptrap (cat house)
of the toothed thighbone (bloodied).

De la douleur minée de l'os
quelque chose naquit
qui devint ce qui fut esprit
pour décaper dans la douleur motrice,
de la douleur,
                cette matrice,
une matrice concrète

                et l'os,
                le fond du tuff
                qui devint os.

From the mined pain of the bone
something was born
which became that which spirit was
to scour in motory pain,
from the pain,

          this matrix,
a concrete matrix

          and the bone,
          the bedrock bottom
          which became bone.

MORALE

Ne te fatigue jamais plus qu'il ne faut, quitte à fonder une culture sur la
fatigue de tes os.

MORAL

Don't tire yourself more than need be, even at the price of founding a
culture on the fatigue of your bones.

MORALE

Quand le tuff fut mangé par l'os,
que l'esprit rongeait par derrière,
l'esprit ouvrit la bouche en trop
et il reçut dans le derrière
                    de la tête
un coup à dessécher ses os;

        alors,

        ALORS,
        alors
        os par os
l'égalisation sempiternelle revint

**et tourna l'atome électrique
avant de fondre point par point.**

MORAL

When the bedrock was eaten by the bone,
that the spirit was gnawing from behind,
the spirit opened too much mouth
and received on the back
                of its head
a bone-withering blow;

                then,

                THEN,
                then
                bone by bone
the sempiternal equalization returned

**and turned the electric atom
before point by point melting down.**

CONCLUSION

Pour moi, simple
Antonin Artaud,
on ne me la fait pas à l'influence
quand on n'est qu'un homme
ou que
              dieu.

Je ne crois à ni père
              ni mère,

ja na pas
a papa-mama,

nature,
esprit
ou dieu,
satan
ou corps
ou être,
vie
ou néant,

CONCLUSION

For me, simple
Antonin Artaud,
no one can bamboozle me with influence
when one is nothing but a man
or nothing but

         god.

I believe in neither father
         nor mother,

ain't gotta
daddy-mommy

nature,
spirit,
or god,
satan
or body
or being,
life
or nothingness,

rien qui soit dehors ou dedans
et surtout pas la bouche d'être,
trou d'un égout foré de dents
où se regarde tout le temps
l'homme qui tète sa substance
en moi,
pour me prendre un papa-maman,
et se refaire une existence
libre de moi
sur mon cadavre
ôté
du vide
même,

et reniflé

        de temps

        en temps.

Je dis

        de par-dessus

        le temps

comme si le temps
n'était pas frite,
n'était pas cette cuite frite
de tous les effrités
du seuil,
réembarqués dans leur cercueil.

nothing that is outside or inside
and above all not the mouth of being,
sewer hole drilled with teeth
where he's always watching himself
the man who sucks his substance
in me,
to take a daddy-mommy from me,
and remake an existence
free of me
on my cadaver
removed
from the void
itself,

and sniffed

         from time
         to time.

I say

         from above
         time

as if time
were not a French fry,
were not this crocked fry
of all the friablized
of the threshold,
reembarked in their coffin.

FROM

INTERJECTIONS

When I eat, the gluttonous void of the bottom of the throat,
of the greedy orifice,
summons the alimentary bolus to monopolize it to the detriment of the
    teeth and the tongue,
with which the uvula from behind has strange complicities.
But all that is of no interest of any kind,
for the tongue
is an obscene hooker who in front is ready to follow the teeth in their
    detailed work of mastication,
and behind,
even more ready to let herself be gobbled by the orifice,
and to push lewdly and treacherously food toward the orifice,

                    the tongue,
pregnant with all her ancestral sagacity,
and which moreover descends from her like a light of the holy spirit.
The so-called apostles, on the day called Pentecost, forty days after the
    flight of Christ facing the martyrdom of Golgotha and the revolt-
    ing death of the authentic martyr of Golgotha (who was called
    Artaud like myself, and I do believe it was me),
believed they saw tongues land on them, enter into them,
but in fact they were not seeing them there, nor from there,
no longer being there,
not yet being there,

having never been there,

they saw again the vast scene of pregenital pigwash where the body of
man, not satisfied with having a chunk of blood sausage between
his thighs, wanted to have another one between his teeth,

where the tongue could coat and lubricate the detonations of speech as
well as the machine-gunning of I know not what mythic dental
anger at the aggressive rush of food,

said thus, amid the cave-ins of invading nourishment, under the unflag-
ging carronades of teeth, there are mephitic trenches of gas,
appalling ravines of hollow matter,

strange molecular wells, amid the rushes of food,

but the entrance of the tongue changed all that,

mastication passed onto the level of the simple micturition of a stupid
erotic masturbation.

Wednesday 27 November 1946 at twenty-three hours in the evening,
beings that have not swallowed the nail,
but have swallowed the point,
and have held themselves between the hard and the soft,

those one cannot disintricate
because if one looks for them in the breath
they take refuge in the body,
and if one looks for them at one point on the body
they claim to be braided there in breath,
lightning gashing the body
like a negation of body,
having more body than all breath.

They collect in the body,
outside of the one who controls this body
and for them has not left it,
being neither intelligent enough to reign over its mental nature,
nor sufficiently this suffering body to be all this body,
in time, the extent of time,
nor old enough in itself to be as old as this body,
nor vegetatively ingenerate enough to be all this innate body,
nor antecedently
                im-planted enough

to be what this body
        is,
nor instinctively
        supple enough
to be its sempiternal ascent,
and which, to finally flee the whip,
takes refuge not in being or life,
heart, soul, consciousness, mind,
but in the strength of the body itself,
latent, in the process of rising,
not in pure volition,
but in lightning or the whip,
in the surface inert in fact,
in the flagellation of fact,
in the reputation between fact and surface,
the depths of the erected
surface (it's the super-brother of detecting)
in the etection of the surface
the thickness of the incorporated is made,
the inert of the body raised by it,
of the body in the process of getting up,
the thickness of the body in tapult, projected by catapult,
molar that volition extracted from itself like an evil.

Ideas don't come without limbs, and so these are no longer ideas but
   limbs, limbs fighting among themselves.

The mental world was never anything but that which remains from a
   hellish trampling of organs while the man who wore them is no
   more.

It is thought from below which leads,
there is no criterion of spirit, of judgement,
spirit is no longer anything but an adventitious memory,
the more a body is a body, the farther it is from spirit and from its con-
   sciousness,
and the more merit it has in body,
and the more the idea of merit escapes,
with its value and its quality,
and the more the life of the body proper prevents it from differentiating
   itself
against value and quality
between value and quality,
and drives to despair the quality of existing;
and the more the body radiates wholly in the oblivion of intrinsic value,
and of the spirit of quality,
and the more it radiates and becomes concrete,
in that the body wanted to squeeze itself out and collect, in order to

become wholly body, in the hatred of spirituality.
The principle of she-yoga is seated on the eternal happiness of swallow-
ing the pain of others.

What body is is the emaciation of the matter of oneself,
achieved by oneself;
what has not been achieved in the pain of the self
falls at the hour of death,
until becoming pure spirit, and that a part of the body becomes the evil
matter of pure spirit.

> **lo menedi**
> **bardar**
> **ta zerubida**
>
> **lo menedida**
> **bardar**
> **la ter**
> **tupi**
> **bahelechi**
> **bertoch**
>
> **na menezucht**
> **bordi**
> **menucht**
> **saba**
> **dezuda**
>
> **dezuda ravi**

Thus perish the spirits of all those who have never wanted to take the
trouble of having a body, and want in spite of everything to have the
freedom of the city under the reign of truly solidified bodies.

For nothing bestializes a being like the taste for eternal happiness, the
search for eternal happiness at any price, and miss Lucifer is that
whore who never wanted to leave eternal happiness.

But now the old cosmic prospection of god will no longer occur.

The famous total dimension is to become as a simple man as strong as
all infinity.

What's going to happen is that men are going to show their instincts
      repressed for so long,
and I my true language;

> **a ta aishena**
> **shoma**
> **shora**
> **borozi**
> **bare**

a cane of red ulcer
with a fart fiber penis.

> **opotambo**
> **zorim**
> **nietecta**
> **opotembech ari nicto**

And the nail will remain nail throughout all eternity, when the Portici
      she-mute of my sensations passes and my body remains intact.

> **insulpici de talpiquante**
> **a la piquante e salapice**

Thus it is that the processional serpent of all bodies, with its mask of red
    spasm, falls to the ground beneath my feet;
and this mask it came back to me, as though not having deserved it.

And I said in the middle of the void,
void of the seven eternities:
The self is not the body, it is the body that is the self.

The Mass grips the Orient like the Occident,
more the Orient where it does not take place than the Occident where
    it does,
the proofs being that it is to the extreme point of the summit of the
    Himalayas that the obscene priests of Rome, Jerusalem and
    Lebanon
will have to go to finish guzzling the benefice of their daily assassina-
    tions of the human body.

            archina
            ne coco rabila
            co rabila
            e caca rila

            archeta
            ne capsa rifila
            ca rifila
            e carta chila

            archita
            ne corto chifila

**corti fila
e capsa chila**

Translation:
Haven't they decorticated the patibulary
cavities of my skull enough
and drawn down the burned hides
of their million damned souls
upon themselves.

The Mass rests on the human orifice,
it takes place on the slope of that bone,
through which man a deloused virgin
pukes.

Man holds the stolen stone at a certain place of the skull,
for his own it is a window (a way of being open to being),
for mine it is the niched stone,
this stone has an aura which is being,
and it is in the aura of being,
the intregal aura of being, the tide of inexhaustible will,
is it will itself, or its rape?
It is the rape of will that created this psychic sea in which every being
     believes it is agitated,
and agitating,
it is thought, that aqueous stone that drags along like the cast-offs of the
     most sordid mendicity,
yes, thought is that obscene hooker who always wants to get screwed,
and who vampirizes in order to get it first,

and every man is that evil thought,
which pretends to be spirit, science, when it doesn't have a body,
when it is only that foul body, rotten, syphilitic, full of sarcoptids,
green with pustules,
that man alone can split hairs over,
that foul mangy gristle, packed with rats and old farts, I mean old sins.
Now, I've never believed in sin, but looking at man today I feel quite
    inclined to think it over again.

Friday 13 December 1946,
the espousals of my rondelles,
testicular, infantile rondelles,
through the palpatory,
intellectual lips
of the lama,
have not yet set fire to *that:*
have not even set fire in me:

they made my daughter Ana come out
of the charnel house of donkey piss beings,

the rampart opposite the beings that emerge from a point blossoming on
    the reverse side of bodies;
and for one night that's already something.

ANTONIN ARTAUD

Compenetration,
penetration,
my language,
melange,
my language,
coming together,

no space,
no infinity,
no far away,
no register,
no ensemble,
no in general,
no total,
no harmony;

everything downstream
but not me,

no contact,

no brushing against,
no coming together,
no penetration,

no compenetration,
no copulation,
     pulation.

To bring into contact
the principle molecules
and to force them
to break one upon the other
the cunt, sworn
by means of a series of repeated propulsions
which obey the tempo of a dance
of which the sexual act
is only a bestial
and aborted caricature.

Now I'm the father-mother,
neither father nor mother,
neither man nor woman,

I've always been there,
always been body,
always been man.

Things are not seen from the height of the spirit over the body
but made by the body,
and on its level,
far more infinite than that of any spirit.

Without law
other than
that of an
extremely
tenebrous,
scrupulous
and obstinate
equity.

Not to forget
the mug
of Lucifer
beneath his Father Eternal
make-up,
sneering through the bars.

Electricity is a body, a weight,
the pestling of a face,
the compressed magnet of a repressed surface from the outside of a
    blow,
at the outskirts of this blow,
blue fist blow of my green hand of despair and anger, one day that
facing this blow
the hole that I was going to deliver to things
snapped up my hand
not to stay clear of an attack
but to be the master,
at last.

They bore holes,

they do more than hollow out notions, values,

they stifle slowly calculated proposals, like one says that a wound sup-
purates,

they do not raise themselves from their body

to enter consciousness,

for what is the spirit without the body?

A dishrag of dead jism.

They do not enter into the "mentous," they do not believe there is a body
called intelligence or science,

anymore than a body named god,

for they no longer see anything in the heavens,

then they understand the heavens,

they no longer believe that things are a void crossed by animal ideas,

they only understand what we do not understand,

and understand that we can no longer understand and perceive what we
see,

for the body is too cramped there,

but the body is not over there, in the future that it swells with all that it
will be,

and it is perhaps in fact thus that god took man's property from him
who, like god, does not exist, there where he has not yet made him-
self,

it is only god who can be made there where he has never worked, at making himself, nor at existing,

thus it is that, not having worked, god took from humanity and its future, and its past.

The seeds were ill-planted.

I don't know what he did, or from where he came out to kill, infect and assassinate,

but my brain is not sick over it, no, my brain is carved by this lowly coal-trimmer work that god night and day indulges in on my corpse of humanity, the remains of my body hunted down from everywhere by the luxuriant vegetation of all the microbes, all the cheese mites, and the crab lice by means of which god eats me, thus probing me thoroughly,

because there isn't just god, but men on the carcass of Artaud the cunt.

ANTONIN ARTAUD

The extreme point of mysticism,
I hold it now in the real and in my body,
like a toilet broom.

For me, living man, I am a city besieged by the army of the dead,
intercepted by their charnel houses,
cut off from all external objects, while I am the external of a dead man,
me,
and those who attack me
are outside,
and it is in the inside that they agitate,
it is in the inside of my body that they cut the thread of the nervous
     antenna, through which I must scold their bodies.
(Old cinematography of catastrophy with which *the illusion* still dresses
     me,
prompted by old escapees from hell,
giving man another bread to browse;
for the bread with which I am ulcerated at this time is that of the infa-
     mous eroticism that beings hurl at me.)

I strike a blow,
the other, from inside my body, at the farthest exterior of the earth
     responds to it with. an imbeciling fluid,
crossed with the abject cross of beings who do not know who has made
     time and who,

beings draw themselves from my interior,

but to what extent?

I will do it again and again,
this man,
on you,
Antonin Artaud,
said god,
the universal god of beings,
always incorrigibly foul,
and always incorrigibly there,
and who says to you:
Take that, take that,
you didn't get me out of there yet,
I'm always there no matter what you try to do,
you haven't defeated me and I have that:
caca, the cream of your. . .
it is me who gobbles up the cake you made crumb by crumb,
and I made a child out of it,
to put him in your place,
maybe one day I'll gobble him up too, unless he has a better way than
      you, and knows to bite me where I stew.

With what will I fill nothingness?

Waiting for the specter flattened against me who melts with each blow
      I strike to finish his delirium.

And not like god,
but like, being, me,
this unique body,
from where all,
even god, came out,
that I have been violated for life,
insulted, offended, dirtied,
polluted, muddied, smutted,
day and night,
since I am alive,

no man at the end of his tether
who does not know how to find in Artaud
something to remake an existence with;

that I have been a little bit everywhere martyrized;

and as to be prevented from being god that I was stabbed in the back, in
    Marseilles,
stabbed in Paris,
received an iron bar blow on the spinal column in Dublin;
as being convicted of being god
and to preclude me, me, from remembering it

that I have been everywhere assassinated, poisoned, beaten to death,
    electrocuted,

and in order to prevent me from finding consciousness again and the
    science of my capacities and my strength

and to defend myself against my persecutors;

for god is called by its real name Artaud, and the name of this kind of
    unnamable thing between the abyss and nothingness,

which partakes of the nature of the abyss and nothingness,

and that one does not call or name,

and it seems that it is a body too,

and that Artaud is a body too,

not the idea, but the fact of the body,

and the fact that what is nothingness is the body,

the unsoundable abyss of the face, of the inaccessible plan of the surface,
    through which the abyss body shows itself;

the Tibetans, the Mongols, the Afghans listening to god

or that the abyss the infinite talks to them,

sounding

the bewildered lair of the knot through which the unconscious heart
    liberates its own thirst from being before what we call nothingness,

say having heard in themselves rise up the syllables of this vocable:

AR-TAU.

A few initiates wanted to plead that it was there the designation of a
    force but not that of an individual,

but not an initiate, in reality, who did not know that this force was that
    of a man and who did not want to chain this man to forbid him to

exist, even if it entails assassinating him later.

And in reality no initiate who did not know that Antonin Artaud, born in Marseilles September 4th 1896, was really that man who, at the bottom of nothingness, was sleeping.

So then it is in prevention from being god
that I,
Antonin Artaud,
have been martyrized eternally,

and as being exactly this man, and the man who never wanted any god,
and whom all the churches have always persecuted to extirpate his athe-
    ism from him,

and it is in prevention from being god that I, Antonin Artaud, petit-
    bourgeois from Marseilles, September 4th, 1896, have seen myself
    stabbed in the back on June 10th, 1916, in Marseilles in front of the
    church of the Reformed,
asphyxiated by spells throughout my entire existence,
stabbed in 1928 in Montmartre a second time in the back,
then struck in Dublin with an iron bar on the spinal column,
attacked on a ship, with in front the anchor hole wide open to let my
    body through,
straight-jacketed on the same ship after the attack,
then interned,
maintained seventeen days in straight jacket with feet attached to the
    bed,
kept three years in solitary confinement,
poisoned systematically for five months,
that I have suffered one month of coma under the shock of the last poi-

soning, in the Sainte-Anne asylum,

finally subjected to two years of electroshock in the Rodez asylum to
lose in it the memory of my so-called supranatural self,

even though I never had two self, but one only, mine, that of a man who
never wanted to hear talk of god.

Then.

Then?

It is in prevention from being god that I have been a little everywhere
persecuted as a man throughout all my life,

here,

but I knew about it only a very short time before the beginning of my
internment,

that it was because all people believed me, me, to be this man,

suspected me of being this body,

had identified me as being this body of man from where all life came
out,

and in prevention from being this body

in which everyone always served himself

without using entrance or exit,

and felt capable of supplying himself,

and which he believed could be used to answer all his needs,

in prevention from being this body charged to provide for all the needs,

and pillaged to the point of plague,

for there is no plague nor cholera, smallpox nor syphilis,

that the succubate,

well-organized,

cannot explain.

It is in prevention from being god
that I am day and night flooded with the sea of succubus jism,
maintained in the gaseous placenta of the seminal alluvium of the water
    mothers, with which one hundred billion harpies every night smear
    my conscience to maintain me in this life,
the world it is water, air, earth, fire, aether,
but it is also the arch-ponderable of all that has always been hidden
and which is this sea of miasmas ja,
of obscene corporal suppurations
which paralyze all will;

everybody gets hauled over the coals,
but there is there a kind of ignoble tenderness
with which I am particularly favored.

I have seen myself in 1915 prey to strange phenomena.

I know now where they were coming from,
for it is in prevention from being god that I am every night honored
    with the visits of one hundred thousand vampires etc.,
and it is because my body is *good* that it is always meticulously visited.

The current plan
(against sleep and art)
of the little Sufi multifolded in a humbug of acrid cow-dung,
for all poison is a sexual plexus.

I do not know anything more than my sensibility of all the seconds,
those of the moments when I feel most myself and most *intensely* present,
    awake, willful and *warned.*
What I know best about myself is my inalienable will, infinite as the
    volume or the plain of my whole body impossible to pierce.
And concerning this point anyone or no one could care less, ever, about
    another offense;
it being understood that the body of Artaud
which contains in the innate state
all that which serves to make that from which the life of silt is born;
it is from this body that they draw
something to remake reality,
something to remake themselves in reality, and to make for themselves
    a reality;
whoever has squandered too much of his blood, of his sperm, of his
    saliva, or of the snot from his nose,
it is inside Artaud that he comes to rebutter:
and the Tower of Butter in Tibet

is the sign of this hold of beings
on that which composes my flesh to be eaten,
is like the perpetual pig of the barometer of how much of my butter is
    needed by beings, to remain in reality.

I have perhaps a thousand friends in the spheres,
in fact perhaps ten living men
who have forgotten that it was done,
who no longer knew what it was all about,
and on what life is centered,
with which crime against Artaud buried,
masturbated and annihilated,
life has always sustained itself.
I have to say to all those friends
that if beings have never forgotten how to approach Artaud by magic,
how to draw saliva from his mouth, and his shit from his coccyx, and his
    sperm under his pubis,
how, from which hollow blubber lips
to turn the night around his bed,
from which opening of the teguments,
from which monstrous dilation of the pores, from which sanious flay-
    ings of tissues under the teguments,
to leech onto all that is him in order to suck him bone dry,
and it is in this way that Antonin Artaud feels his testicles suppurate
in the middle of which a thousand heads circulate having perched their
    paradise there,
vying with one another to sneer at him, if he does not disclose immedi-
    ately where the bad spirit is lodged, which came right up to him;

— And where I am, you don't know where I am, nor how I arrived
   here.

It is in this way that they swallow Artaud, that they suck him off, that
   they defecate him, that they lick him and lick their chops with him,
in this way throughout life;
and if Antonin Artaud complains,
that means *he* is delirious;
quick, a little electroshock to cure him of believing in spirits;
but it is precisely that Antonin Artaud does not believe in spirits, but
   that he has always believed in men,
who have never known how to do anything else to buttress their igno-
   ble lives than to come back to life in him,
and it is in order for that not to be known and to pursue their hideous
   profits in peace,
that they had Artaud put to bed,
completely naked, in a cell, held secretly for three years,
and had him poisoned and convicted of madness,
so that he would not be able to revolt
and so that nobody would think to help him.
But Artaud can do without men, and it is all by himself that he got his
   liberty back.

For magic to enter into Artaud,
it's magic to croak in Artaud,
and that's the way that Antonin Artaud took his enemies prisoners,
for I, Antonin Artaud, for nine years convicted of delirium and mad-
   ness, I now performed magic.

I performed it for three years in Rodez, I had performed it for three
    years in Ville-Evrard, before Rodez,

and those were the sniffings and whirlings for which the doctors
    reproached me.

As for magic, I take in my thick breath, and by means of my nose, of my
    mouth, of my hands and of my feet I project it against everything
    that obstructs me.

And how many boxes, chests, totems, grigri, partitions, surfaces, sticks,
    nails, ropes, and a hundred nails, breastplates, helmets, armor plat-
    ings, masks, carders, iron collars, winches, garrots, gibbets and
    dials, are there now in the air

by my will projected.

I will tell you that when I will have made society give back the billion
    tons of cocaine and heroin it stole from me, — with the aid of nine
    small pneumatic cannons, and the cane that I have forged.

Me, Artaud,
worked over,
to rid me of evil,

but why not know when it will end.

I cannot know what I will do tomorrow,
I do not want to know,
but I want to know that evil will end immediately.
No, it will never end either.
So.
I am the master of the elements
and the one of events.
I don't want to be touched anymore,
                  invaded
as I am by others,
I don't want to be put to sleep by others,
sleep is an illusion in which one continues to live.

I don't want these death pangs anymore.

I don't want to sleep anymore.

I don't want to die.

I don't want to dream anymore.

THE HUMAN FACE

The human face is an empty force, a field of death.

The old revolutionary demand for a form which has never corresponded to its body, which left to be something other than the body.

So it's absurd to reproach a painter for being academic who now still persists in reproducing the features of the human face as they are; for as they are they still have not found the form that they indicate and specify; and do more than sketch, but from morning to night, and in the midst of ten thousand dreams, pound as in the crucible of a never-tiring impassioned palpitation.

Which means that the human face has not yet found its face.

and that it's up to the painter to give it one. But this means that the human face as it is is still searching with two eyes, a nose, a mouth and two auricular cavities which correspond to the holes of orbits like the four openings of the burial vault of approaching death.

The human face bears in fact a kind of perpetual death on its face

from which it's up to the painter precisely to save it

in giving its own features back to it.

For the thousands and thousands of years in fact that the human face has been speaking and breathing

one somehow still has the impression that it has not yet started to say what it is and what it knows.

And I don't know of any painter in the history of art from Holbein to Ingres, who, this face of man, succeeded in making it speak. The portraits by Holbein or Ingres are thick walls which explain nothing about the ancient mortal architecture which buttresses itself under the arcs of the eyelids' vault, or embeds itself in the cylindrical tunnel of the two mural cavities of the ears.

Only van Gogh was able to draw out of a human head a portrait which was the explosive rocket of the beating of a buried heart.

His own.

Van Gogh's head in a soft felt hat renders null and void all the attempts of abstract paintings which can be made after him, until the end of eternities.

For this face of an avid butcher, projected like cannon shot onto the most extreme surface of the canvas,

and which all of a sudden sees itself stopped

by an empty eye

and returned toward the inside,

completely exhausts the most specious secrets in which abstract or nonfigurative painting can delight,

which is why, in the portraits I have drawn,

I have above all avoided forgetting the nose, the mouth, the eyes, the ears or the hair, but I've tried to make this face that was speaking to me tell

the secret

of an old human story which passed as if dead in the heads of Ingres or Holbein.

Sometimes, next to human heads, I've made objects, trees or animals appear because I'm still not sure of the limits at which the body of the human self can stop.

Moreover I've definitely broken with art, style or talent in all the drawings that you will see here. I want to say that there will be hell to pay for whoever considers them works of art, works of aesthetic stimulation of reality.

Not one is properly speaking a work.

All are sketches, I mean soundings or staggering blows in all directions of chance, possibility, luck, or destiny.

I have not sought to refine my lines or my results,

but to express certain kinds of patent linear truths which have as much value thanks to words, written phrases, as graphic style and the perspective of features.

It is thus that several drawings are mixtures of poems and portraits, of written interjections and plastic evocations of elements, of materials, of personages, of men or animals.

It is in that way that one must accept these drawings in the barbarism and the disorder of their graphic style "which is never preoccupied with art" but with the sincerety and spontaneity of the line.

TO HAVE DONE WITH THE JUDGEMENT OF GOD

kré	Everything must	**puc te**
kré	be arranged	**puk te**
pek	to a hair	**li le**
kre	in a fulminating	**pek ti le**
e	order.	**kruk**
pte		

I learned yesterday

(you must think that I'm very slow, or perhaps it is only a false rumor,
some of the dirty gossip that is peddled between the sink and the
latrines at the hour when the buckets are filled with meals once
again regurgitated),

I learned yesterday

about one of the most sensational official practices of the American pub-
lic schools

which no doubt make that country consider itself at the head of
progress.

Apparently, among the examinations or tests that a child has to undergo
on entering a public school for the first time is the one called the
seminal liquid or sperm test,

which consists of asking this newly-enrolled child for a little of his
sperm in order to put it into a glass jar

and of thereby keeping it ready for all the attempts at artificial insemi-
nation which might eventually take place.

For more and more the Americans find that they lack manpower and
children,

that is, not workers

but soldiers,

and at all costs and by all possible means they want to make and manu-
facture soldiers

in view of all the planetary wars which might subsequently take place,

and which would be destined to *demonstrate* by the crushing virtues of
force
the superexcellence of American products,
and the fruits of American sweat in all the fields of activity and poten-
tial dynamism of force.
Because there must be production,
nature must be replaced wherever it can be replaced by every possible
means of activity,
a major field must be found for human inertia,
the worker must be kept busy at something,
new fields of activity must be created,
where all the false manufactured products,
all the ignoble synthetic ersatzes will finally reign,
where beautiful true nature has nothing to do,
and must give up its place once and for all and shamefully to all the tri-
umphant replacement products,
where sperm from all the artificial insemination factories
will work miracles
to produce armies and battleships.
No more fruit, no more trees, no more vegetables, no more plants phar-
maceutical or not and consequently no more food,
but synthetic products to repletion,
in vapors,
in special humors of the atmosphere, on particular axes of atmospheres
drawn by force and by synthesis from the resistance of a nature that
has never known anything about war except fear.
And long live war, right?
For by doing this, it is war, isn't it, that the Americans have prepared for
and that they prepare for thus step by step.

To defend this insane machining against all the competition which
    would inevitably break out on all sides,
there must be soldiers, armies, airplanes, battleships,
therefore this sperm
which the American governments have apparently had the nerve to
    consider.
For we have more than one enemy
and one who watches us, kid,
us, the born capitalists,
and among these enemies
Stalin's Russia
which is not short of armed men either.
All this is very fine,
but I did not know that the Americans were such a warlike people.
To fight you must receive blows
and perhaps I have seen many Americans at war
but in front of them they always had incommensurable armies of tanks,
    planes, battleships
serving as a shield.
I saw a lot of machines fight
but I saw only in the infinite
              rear
the men who drove them.
Confronted by a people who make their horses, oxen and donkeys eat
    the last tons of true morphine which may be left to them in order to
    replace it with ersatz smoke,
I prefer the people who eat right out of the earth the delirium that gave
    birth to them,
I am speaking of the Tarahumaras

who eat Peyote straight from the soil
while it is born,
and who kill the sun in order to establish the kingdom of black night,
and who split the cross so that the spaces of space will never again meet
    or cross.

In this way you will hear the dance of the TUTUGURI.

TUTUGURI

THE RITE OF THE BLACK SUN

And below, as at the bottom of the bitter,
cruelly desperate slope of the heart,
the circle of the six crosses opens,
                    far below,
as if embedded in the mother earth,
disembedded from the filthy embrace of the mother
                    who slobbers.

The earth of black coal
is the only humid spot
in this cleft of rock.

The Rite is that the new sun passes through seven points before explod-
    ing at the earth's orifice.

And there are six men,
one for each sun,
and a seventh man
who is the sun completely
                    raw

dressed in black and red flesh.

Now, this seventh man
is a horse,
a horse with a man leading him.

But it is the horse
that is the sun
and not the man.

On the rending of a drum and of a long, peculiar
trumpet,
the six men
who were lying down,
rolled up flush with the ground,
spring up successively like sunflowers,
not suns at all
but turning soils,
lotuses of water,
and to each upspring
corresponds the increasingly gloomy and *repressed*
        gong
        of the drum
until suddenly we see coming in full gallop, at vertiginous speed,
the last sun,
the first man,
the black horse with a
        man naked,
        absolutely naked

and *virgin*
on it.

Having gamboled, they advance following circular meanders
and the horse of bloody meat panics
and caracoles without stopping
on the top of its rock
until the six men
have finished encircling
completely
the six crosses.

Now, the major tone of the Rite is precisely
THE ABOLITION OF THE CROSS.

Having finished turning
they uproot
the earthen crosses
and the man naked
on the horse
raises high
an immense horseshoe
which he has tempered in a cut of his blood.

RESEARCH ON FECALITY

There where it smells of shit
it smells of being.
Man could very well have avoided shitting,
and kept his anal pocket closed,
but he chose to shit
like he could've chosen to live
instead of consenting to live dead.

The fact is that in order not to make caca,
he would've had to consent
not to be,
but he could not resolve to lose
         being,
in other words to die alive.

There is in being
something particularly tempting for man
and that something is precisely
        CACA
      (Roarings here.)

In order to exist you need only let yourself go to be,
but to live,
you must be somebody,
to be somebody,
you must have a BONE,
not be afraid of showing the bone,
and of losing the meat on the way.

Man has always preferred meat
to the earth of bones.
The fact is there was only earth and bone wood,
and he had to earn his meat,
there was only iron and fire
and no shit,
and man was afraid of losing shit
or rather he *desired* shit
and, for that, sacrificed blood.

In order to have shit,
in other words meat,
where there was only blood
and the scrap iron of bones
and where there was no question of earning being
but where there was one of losing life.

       o reche modo
       to edire
       di za

ANTONIN ARTAUD

**tau dari
do padera coco**

There, man withdrew and fled.

Then the beasts ate him.

It was not a rape,
he lent himself to the obscene meal.

He found it tasty,
even he himself learned
to play the beast
and to eat rat
daintily.

And where does this filthy abasement come from?

From the fact that the world is not yet formed,
or from the fact that man has only a faint idea of the world
which he wants to keep forever?

That comes from the fact that man,
one fine day,
stopped
the idea of the world.

Two roads were offered to him:
that of the infinite outside,

that of the infinitesimal inside.

And he chose the infinitesimal inside.
Where it is only a question of squeezing
the rat,
the tongue,
the anus
or the glans.

And god, god himself hastened the movement.

Is god a being?
If he is it is made of shit.
If he is not
he's not.
Now, he is not,
but like the void which advances with all its forms
of which the most perfect representation
is the march of an incalculable group of crab lice.

"You are mad, Mr. Artaud, and the Mass?"

I abjure baptism and the Mass.
There is no human act
which, on the internal erotic plane,
is more pernicious than the descent
of so-called Jesus christ
onto the altars.

No one will believe me
and from here I see the public shrugging its shoulders
but the named christ is no other than he
who facing the crab louse god
consented to live without a body,
while an army of men
descended from a cross,
where god believed he had long ago nailed them,
rebelled,
and, cased in iron,
in blood,
in fire, and bones,
advances, reviling the Invisible
in order to end GOD'S JUDGEMENT there.

To Raise the Question Of. . .

What is serious
is that we know
that after the order
of this world
there is another.

Which is it?

We do not know.

The number and order of possible suppositions in this domain
is precisely
infinity!

And what is infinity?

We do not exactly know!

It is a word
we employ
to indicate

the opening
of our consciousness
towards an immeasurable
possibility,
indefatigable and immeasurable.

And what exactly is consciousness?

We do not exactly know.

It is nothingness.

A nothingness
we employ
to indicate
when we do not know something
from what side
we do not know it
and we say
then
consciousness,
from the side of consciousness,
but there are a hundred thousand other sides.

So what?

It seems that consciousness
is in us
linked

to sexual desire
and hunger;

but it could
very well
not be
linked to them.

It is said,
it can be said,
there are those who say
that consciousness
is an appetite,
the appetite for life;

and immediately
beside the appetite for life,
it is the appetite for food
which comes immediately to mind;

as though there were not people who eat
without any kind of appetite;
and who are hungry.

For that also
occurs
to be hungry
without appetite;

so what?

So

the space of possibility
was given me one day
like a loud fart
that I will let;

but neither the space,
nor the possibility,
I didn't know exactly what they were,

and I didn't feel the need to think about it,

they were words
invented to define things
which existed
or did not exist
confronted by
the pressing urgency
of a need:
that of abolishing the idea,
the idea and its myth,
and of enthroning in its place
the thundering manifestation
of this explosive necessity:
to dilate the body of my internal night,

of the internal nothingness
of my self

which is night,
nothingness,
irreflection,

but which is an explosive assertion
that there is
something
to make way for:

my body.

And really
reduce my body to
this stinking gas?
To say that I have a body
because I have a stinking gas
which forms
inside me?

I don't know
but
I do know that

        space,
        time,
        dimension,
        becoming,

the future,
the hereafter,
being,
non-being,
the self,
the non-self,
are nothing to me;

but there is one thing
which is something,
only one thing
which is something,
and I feel it
because it wants to
COME OUT:
the presence
of my corporal
pain,

the menacing,
never tiring
presence
of my
body;

however much I am pressed with questions
and deny all questions,
there is a point
where I find myself forced

to say no,
>   NO

then
to negation;

and this point,
it's when I'm pressed,

when I'm squeezed out
and am milked
until the departure
within me
of food,
of my food
and its milk,

and what remains?

That I am suffocated;

and I don't know if it is an action
but by pressing me thus with questions
even to the absence
and the nothingness
of the question
I was pressed
even to the suffocation
within me

of the idea of body
and of being a body,

and it is then that I smelled the obscene

and that I farted
out of folly
and out of excess
and out of the revolt
of my suffocation.

The fact is I was being pressed
right up to my body
and right up to the body

and it is then
that I shattered everything
because my body
is never to be touched.

CONCLUSION

— And what has been your purpose, Mr. Artaud, in this radio broadcast?

— In principle to denounce a certain number of officially consecrated and acknowledged social filths:

1° this emission of infantile sperm given free of charge by children with a view to the artificial insemination of foetuses still to be born that will see the light of day in a century or more.

2° To denounce, in this same American people who occupy the entire surface of the former Indian continent, a revival of the warlike imperialism of ancient America which caused the pre-Columbian Indians to be despised by all precedent mankind.

3° — You are expressing here, Mr. Artaud, some very bizarre things.

4° — Yes, I am saying something bizarre,
the fact is that the pre-Columbian Indians were, contrary to whatever one might have believed, a strangely civilized people
who had in fact known a form of civilization based on the exclusive principle of cruelty.

5° — And do you know exactly what cruelty is?

6° — Just like that, no, I don't know.

7° — Cruelty, it's to extirpate through the blood and as far as the blood god, the bestial risk of unconscious human animality, wherever it may be encountered.

8° — Man, when he is not held back, is an erotic animal,
he has within him an inspired tremor,
a sort of pulsation
producing innumerable beasts which are the form the ancient terrestrial peoples universally attributed to god.
That made what is called a spirit.
Now, this spirit which came from the American Indians is reappearing a little bit everywhere today in scientific guise which serves only to reveal this spirit's morbid infectuous hold, the salient state of vice, but a vice pullulating with diseases,
for, laugh as much as you wish,
what have been called microbes
is in fact god,
and do you know what the Americans and the Russians make their atoms with?
They make them with the microbes of god.

— You are raving, Mr. Artaud.
You are mad.

— I am not raving.

I'm not mad.

I'm telling you that microbes have been reinvented in order to impose a
new idea of god.

A new way has been found to make god come out again and to catch
him in the act of his microbial noxiousness.

It's to nail him to the heart,

there where men love him best,

in the form of sickly sexuality,

in that sinister guise of morbid cruelty which he dons in the hours when
it pleases him as it does now to tetanize and madden humanity.

He uses the spirit of purity of a consciousness that has remained ingen-
uous like mine to asphyxiate it with all the false appearances which
he spreads universally through the spaces and it is thus that Artaud
the Mômo can appear to be hallucinating.

— What do you mean, Mr. Artaud?

— I mean that I have found the way to have done once and for all with
this monkey

and that if nobody believes anymore in god everybody believes more
and more in man.

And it is man that we must now decide to emasculate.

— How so?

How so?

From whatever angle one approaches you you are mad, mad enough to
    tie down.

— By having him undergo once more but for the last time an autopsy
    in order to remake his anatomy.
I say, in order to remake his anatomy.
Man is sick because he is badly constructed.
We must decide to strip him in order to scratch out this animalcule
    which makes him itch to death,

        god,
        and with god
        his organs.

For tie me down if you want to,
but there is nothing more useless than an organ.

When you have given him a body without organs,
then you will have delivered him from all his automatisms and restored
    him to his true liberty.

Then you will teach him again to dance inside out
as in the delirium of dance halls
and that inside out will be his true side out.

THE THEATER OF CRUELTY

Do you know anything more outrageously fecal
than the story of god
and of his being: SATAN,
the membrane of the heart
the ignominious sow
of the illusory universal
who with her slobbering udders
has never concealed anything from us
except Nothingness?

Facing this idea of a pre-established universe,
man has never succeeded up to now in establishing his superiority over
    the empires of possibility.

For if there is nothing,
there is nothing,
except this excremental idea
of a being who created for example the beasts.

And where do the beasts come from
in that case?
From the fact that the world of corporal perceptions
is not on its plane,
and not to the point,

from the fact that there is a psychic life
and no true organic life,

from the fact that the simple idea of a pure organic life
can be raised,

from the fact that a distinction
could arise between
embryonically pure organic life
and the impassioned and concretely
integral life of the human body.

The human life is an electric battery
whose discharges have been repelled and castrated,

whose abilities and emphases
have been oriented toward sexual life
while it is made
precisely for absorbing
by its voltaic displacements
all the errant availabilities
of the infinity of the void,
of the increasingly incommensurable
holes of void
of a never fulfilled organic possibility.

The human body needs to eat,
but who has ever tested other than on the plane of sexual life the incom-
     mensurable abilities of the appetites?

Make human anatomy dance at last,

from top to bottom and from bottom to top,
from backward to forward and
from forward to backward,
but much more from backward to backward,
moreover, than from backward to forward,

and the problem of the rarefaction
of foodstuffs
will no longer have to be solved,
because there will no longer be a reason,
even, for raising it.

The human body has been made to eat,
has been made to drink,
in order to avoid
making it dance.

It has been made to fornicate the occult
in order to avoid
grinding down
and executing occult life.

For nothing
deserves to be executed
as much as so-called occult life.

It is there that god and his being
thought to flee from demented man,
there, on that increasingly absent plane of occult life
where god wanted to make man believe
that things could be seen and grasped in spirit,
even though there is nothing existent and real,
except external physical life,
and that all that flees from it and turns away from it
is only the limbo of the demons' world.

And god wanted to make man believe in that reality of the demons'
     world.

But the demons' world is absent.
It will never meet with evidence.
The best way to cure oneself of it
and to destroy it
is to complete the construction of reality.
For reality is not completed,
is not yet constructed.
On its completion will depend
in the world of eternal life
the return of eternal health.

The theater of cruelty
is not the symbol of an absent void,
of an appalling incapacity for realizing itself in human life.
It is the affirmation

of a terrible
and moreover inescapable necessity.

On the never-visited slopes
of the Caucasus,
of the Carpathians,
of the Himalayas,
of the Apennines,
have been conducted everyday,
night and day,
for years and years,
appalling corporal rites
where the black life,
the never restrained and black life
gives itself appalling and repellent meals.

There, the limbs and organs considered vile
because
perpetually vilified,
driven back
outside the rapacities of exterior lyrical life,
are used in all the delirium of unbridled eroticism,
in the midst of the discharge,
increasingly fascinating
and virgin,
of a liquor
whose nature has always refused classification
because it is increasingly increate and impartial.

(It is not especially a question of the sex organ or the anus
which should moreoever be cut off and got rid of,
but of the top of the thighs,
of the hips,
of the loins,
of the entire sexless belly
and of the navel.)

All this is for the moment sexual and obscene
because it has never been possible to work and to cultivate it
outside the obscene
and the bodies that dance there
are undetachable from the obscene,
they have systematically embraced obscene life
but this dance of obscene bodies
must be destroyed
in order to replace them by the dance
of our bodies.

I have been crazed
and tetanized
for years
by the dance of an appalling world of exclusively
sexualized microbes
in which I recognized
in the life of certain repressed spaces
men, women,
children of modern life.

I have been endlessly tormented by the itchings of intolerable eczemas
in which all the purulences of the erotic life of the coffin
flowed at full vent.

There is no need to seek anywhere except in these black ritual dances
the origin of all the eczemas,
all the shingles,
all the tuberculoses,
all the epidemics,
all the plagues
whose cauterization
modern medicine,
increasingly baffled,
proves quite unable to achieve.

My sensibility has been forced to descend,
for ten years,
the steps of the most monstrous sarcophagi,
of the yet unoperated world of the dead
and of the living who have chosen
(and at the point where we are, it's through vice),
who have chosen to live dead.

But I will quite simply have avoided being sick
and with me
a whole world which is everything that I know.

      o pedana
      na komev

tau dedana
tau komev

na dedanu
na komev
tau komev
na come

copsi tra
ka figa arounda

ka lakeou
to cobbra

cobra ja
ja futsa mata

OF THE serpent isn't any of
IT NA

Because you have allowed the organisms to put out their tongues
the organisms' tongues should have been
cut off
at the exit of the body's tunnels.

There is plague,
cholera,
black smallpox
only because the dance

and consequently the theater
have not yet begun to exist.

What doctor of the rationed bodies of present misery has ever sought to
    really examine a cholera?

By listening to the breathing or the pulse of a patient,
by lending an ear, facing the concentration camps of these rationed bod-
    ies of misery,
to the beating of feet, of trunks and sex organs
of the immense and repressed field
of certain terrible microbes
which are
other human bodies.

Where are they?
At ground level or in the depths
of certain tombs
in historically if not geographically
unsuspected places.

> **ko embach**
> **tu ur ja bella**
> **ur ja bella**

> **kou embach**

There, the living make appointments
with the dead

and certain paintings of *danses macabres*
have no other origin.

It is to these upheavals
where the meeting of two extraordinary worlds is unceasingly depicted
that we owe the paintings of the Middle Ages,
as moreover all paintings,
all history
and I will even say
all geography.

The earth is depicted and described
under the action of a terrible dance
to which all its fruits have not yet been
epidemically bestowed.

ANTONIN ARTAUD

POST-SCRIPTUM

There where there is metaphysics,
mysticism,
irreducible dialectics,
I hear the huge
colon of my
hunger writhe
and under the impulses of its somber life
I dictate to my hands
        their dance,
        to my feet
        or to my arms.

The theater and the dance of song
are the theater of the furious rebellions
of the misery of the human body
facing the problems it does not penetrate
or whose passive,
        specious,
        quibbling,
        inscrutable,
        inevident nature
        excedes it.

So it dances
in blocks of
KHA, KHA

infinitely more arid
but organic;

it brings to heel
the black rampart
of the internal liquor's displacements;

the world of invertebrate larvae
which from the endless night
of useless insects breaks away:
       lice,
       fleas,
       bedbugs,
       mosquitos,
       spiders,
occurs only
because the everyday body
has lost under hunger
its primal cohesion
and it loses in gusts,
       in mountains,
       in gangs,
       in endless theories
the black and bitter fumes
of its energy's
rage.

ANTONIN ARTAUD

POST-SCRIPTUM

Who am I?
Where do I come from?
I am Antonin Artaud
and if I say it
as I know how to say it
immediately
you will see my present body
fly into pieces
and under ten thousand
notorious aspects
a new body
will be assembled
in which you will never again
be able
to forget me.

OPEN LETTER

TO THE

REVEREND FATHER LAVAL

Sir,

All that is fine and that you recognize my right to totally and integrally
    express my *individuality*.
However singular it may be
and
heterogeneous it may appear.
But there is one thing you do not say
and which constitutes a fundamental reservation about this right of
    expression,
it is that you yourself were
and are
BOUND by 2
          CAPITAL rites,
that is, when you uttered those words,
you were in reality
BOUND by 2 rites
with your own consent
paralyzing
your hands.
The fact is that like every priest
you were

and are *bound*
by the 2 rites
of the *consecration*
and *elevation*
of the Mass.
The fact is that like every Catholic priest
you had said your Mass that very morning.
And the celebration of the ceremony
called Mass
includes in the foreground
those 2 rites of *binding*
which for me
are tantamount to a downright spell
Consecration
and
elevation
are
spells
     of a special
     but
     MAJOR order
which, if I may say so, capitalizes
     life,
which drains all the spiritual forces in such a direction that all that is
    body is reduced to nothingness
and nothing else remains except a certain
     psychic life
completely freed
but so free

that all the phantasms
of the spirit,
of pure spirit
can be given free rein there
and there occurs
the sinister and torrential expansion of the diluvian and antediluvian
    life
of obsessional beasts
and it is precisely against all this
        that we are struggling
because flagitious sexual life is behind the free expansions of the spirit
and that
is what
the consecration
and
elevation
of the Mass
have
without saying it
        FREED.
There is a nauseating flocculation of the infectious life of being
which the PURE BODY
        repulses
but which
        the PURE SPIRIT
        accepts
and which the Mass
through its rites brings about.
And it is this flocculation

which maintains the present
    life of this world
in the spiritual lower depths
into which it is forever plunging.
But this is what popular consciousness will never understand,
that a macerated and trampled body,
crushed and compiled
by the suffering and pains of being nailed to the cross
like the ever living body of Golgotha
will be superior to a spirit handed over to all the phantasms of the inte-
    rior life
which is merely the leaven
and the seed
for all the stinking phantasmagorical bestializations.

NOTES

The nine works that make up this book are presented in chronological order, as indicated by the datings in the Gallimard Œuvres complètes (henceforth OC). In most cases there are early drafts of these works, and they can be found at the end of the final texts in the Gallimard volumes. These notes are minimal; they are intended to indicate on what basis coined or archaic words were translated, to offer some contextualizing information (not offered in the Introduction), and to point out other sources in Artaud that can be brought to bear on possible obscurities.

ON THE CHIMERAS

OC XI, 1974, pp. 184-201. This text is based on a compilation of several drafts of an unsent letter to the critic Georges Le Breton who had published an essay on Gérard de Nerval ("la Clé des Chimères: l'Alchimie") in the magazine *Fontaine,* spring, 1945. The letter was originally drafted in a notebook, after which passages were copied out and reworked toward a more formal essay.

This letter could be thought of as Artaud's "Defense of Poetry."

For an accurate, readable translation of "les Chimères," see Robert Duncan's version in *Bending The Bow,* New Directions, 1968; reprinted in Gérard de Nerval, *Aurélia and other writings,* Exact Change, 1995. An improvisational version of the work by Robin Blaser is to be found in *The Holy Forest,* Coach House Press, 1993.

"Beingity" is based on Artaud's coined "êtreté" ("être," being, plus the suffix "-té"). For another passage in which the word occurs, see p. 260 of *OC* XIX.

"ama": From the Greek *ame,* which in French is "soul"; sounds the "ama" in "Amalekite" below it in the text. In Latin, "ama" is equivalent to "amula," in the early Christian church the vessel for the wine offered by the people for the Eucharist.

FRAGMENTATIONS

OC XIV*, 1978, pp. 13-22. The text is taken from notebook entries in March, 1946, shortly before Artaud was released from Rodez. It was initially called "Fragments." As he shaped the work, revising it to reflect facets of his "daughters of the heart, to be born," he changed the title to "Fragmentations."

"Yvonne... and little Anie": These "six daughters of the heart, to be born" emerged out of Artaud's regenerative project in Rodez, 1945-1946. Stephen Barber writes:

> These "daughters" were a highly charged, sexually imbued and manipulable group. Artaud usually imagined six daughters for himself, but he could, when necessary, incorporate other women into the existing children. The daughters combined purely imaginative elements with presences from Artaud's past life. Both of his grandmothers became daughters, as did Cécile Schramme, Yvonne Allendy and Anie Besnard. The daughters fought for him, and suffered terrible tortures in their efforts to reach him at Rodez and free him. Artaud was always certain of their imminent arrival. He wrote to Anie Besnard on 29 October 1945: "I am awaiting you as arranged, together with your sister Catherine, for whom I no longer have an address, and Cécile, Yvonne and Neneka. You have suffered far too much for anything to stop you and hold you back this time. . ." Around March 1946, he made a drawing entitled "The theatre of cruelty," which shows four of the daughters in coffins, placed across one another at tangents. Their bodies are scarred and mummified, and they are guarded by an immense, distorted, bird-like creature, but their eyes are open and alert. After his release from Rodez, Artaud wrote to Gilbert Lély, the biographer of the Marquis de Sade, describing the origin of his daughters:
>
> > "I thought a lot about love at the asylum of Rodez, and it was there that I dreamed about some daughters of my soul, who loved me like daughters, and not as lovers — me, their pre-pubescent, lustful, salacious, erotic and incestuous father;
> >
> > "and chaste also, so chaste that it makes him dangerous." (Barber, p. 116)

Yvonne Allendy was an old friend from the late 1920s. Through her and her husband, the psychiatrist, René Allendy, Artaud met Anaïs Nin in 1933. Yvonne Allendy died in 1935.

Marie Chili (1831-1911) and Catherine Chili (1833-1894), born in Tinos (Cyclades) and Smyrna (Turkey), became Artaud's two grandmothers.

Cécile Schramme is the young Belgian who Artaud became infatuated with in the mid-1930s. She died in a sanatorium in Belgium in 1950.

Ana Corbin is only identifiable as someone, according to Artaud, who worked in the Dreyer film, *la Passion de Jeanne d'Arc*.

Anie Besnard, from Luxembourg, was a young friend of Artaud's, whom he met in Paris in the early 30s.

"Ka": "The *ka* was a term for the creative and preserving power of life. In ancient [Egypt] it referred particularly to male potency, hence its phonetic resemblance to the word 'ka' meaning 'bull.' The hieroglyph 'ka' with hands raised in a defensive attitude was a magical gesture designed to preserve the life of the wearer from evil forces. The *ka* accompanied a person like a kind of double, but when the person died the *ka* lived on." (*The Gods and Symbols of Ancient Egypt,* Manfred Lurker, Thames & Hudson, 1984, p. 73)

Elsewhere Artaud spells "ka" as "Kah" or "Kah Kah," punning on "caca." According to Artaud, "ka" as insulin or opium has the power of "caca" without its materiality.

At other points, "ka" is absorbed into longer, apparently coined words ("kaya," "kavina," "dakantala"), which are part of chant constructions.

"tétême": Apparently coined by Artaud; possibly based on "téter" (to suck, as a breast) and "aime" (from "aimer," to love), as well as "t'aime" (I love you). In this passage, "tétême" is quickly linked up with "éma," Artaud's pronunciation of "haimo" (blood, in Greek). "éma" also appears in Artaud's November 17, 1946 letter to Henri Parisot, in a long passage which sheds some light on how Artaud is using it. See Weaver, pp. 476-477.

"té vé": Probably not a reference to TV, but to the Marseilles slang for "bonjour" (good day).

"asses": Artaud has dropped the "l" from "cul" (ass). We have not attempted to match this in English, as the results lead to unfortunate puns: "as" for "ass," or "but" for "butt."

The last two paragraphs of "Fragmentations" introduce two more women friends, both of whom had recently visited Artaud in Rodez. The scholar Marthe Robert (whose books in English translation include *Franz Kafka's Loneliness* and *The Psychoanalytic Revolution*) performed his texts at the Galerie Pierre readings in 1947. Colette Thomas, an actress married to the novelist Henri Thomas, had a background of mental instability and had already spent time in asylums. She performed "Fragmentations" at a theater benefit for Artaud in 1946.

The doctor Jean Dequeker went to work at Rodez in March, 1945. The warmth that he and his wife, Madeleine, showed toward Artaud made his last year there more endurable.

Readers may find fascinating overlays in Artaud's "daughters of the heart" and the American "outsider artist" Henry Darger's 15,000 page saga, "The Story of the Vivian Girls in what is known as The Realms of the Unreal, of the Glandeo-Angelinnean War storm, caused by the Child Slave Rebellion." Written out over the lifetime of this reclusive Chicago artist (who worked as a hospital custodian), Darger's cosmic tale, filled with unusual grammar, rhythmic repetitions, and neologisms, portrays its seven virtuous princesses as innocent, helpless heroines, fighting adult manipulation and violence. Like Artaud's "daughters," the Vivian Girls are repeatedly captured, tortured, and sentenced to death. John M. MacGregor writes: "Darger's personal experience of little girls was limited. In his drawings of them, tracings from published sources, girls are frequently shown naked and usually with male genitals, which he carefully added." ("I see a World within the World: I Dream but am Awake," in *Parallel Visions: Modern Artists and Outsider Art,* Princeton, 1992, pp. 259-270)

LETTER TO PETER WATSON

OC XII, 1974, pp. 230-239. In the summer of 1946, it appeared that two sections from Artaud's poem, "Artaud the Mômo," were to be translated and published in the English magazine, *Horizon.* Peter Watson, the art editor, wrote to Artaud at this time requesting information that would introduce him to the English public. Artaud began his letter in July and completed it in early September. While the letter appears to have been received by Watson, neither it nor the poems appeared in *Horizon.*

"voctrovi. . .": As early as 1943 Artaud was working out "syllable words" in Rodez as part of his self-defense against demons, and probably too as an aggression against them. The first appearance of these syllables in writing that I am aware of is in a March 29, 1943 letter to Ferdière (see Weaver, p. 424), in which Artaud refers to them as a reflection of a "transcendental initiation." In the same letter (p. 427), he argues that part of the poet Ronsard's "sacred Mission was to translate into a language that speaks to the heart the wealth of the things of the Infinite, which are magical and mysterious in their essence. And as such he was, like all true poets, and more than other men, horribly tormented by demons." The syllables do not regularly begin to appear until 1945, when

Artaud suggests they are "attempts at language which must be similar to the language of that old book. But they can only be read rhythmically, in a tempo which the reader himself must find in order to understand and to think." (Weaver, p. 451) The "old book" that Artaud refers to is *Letura d'Eprahi Falli Tetar Fendi Photia o Fotre Indi,* mentioned in the Watson letter as simply *Letura d'Eprahi,* written in 1935, and lost. The effect of the syllables, which generally appear in lines of one to three words, and are then set in regular stanzas, is to physicalize the writing, to give it a vocality, or as Susan Sontag has written, "an unmediated physical presence," that contrasts sharply with the veering fantasy and argument of the text. In a sense, they become the underbelly of the text, or its unseen side, as if turned a bit to the left or to the right it would blur into a roar. These sound blocks appear to be very carefully worked out, with repetitions, semi-repetitions, and variations, offering the individual "sections" a specific identity. While many of the sounds appear to be nonreferential, others appear to relate to existing words. Naomi Greene writes:

> Although it is impossible to analyze most of the words found in Artaud's incantations, certain general remarks can be made. As Eric Sellin notes, many words reflect Artaud's preoccupations: papa, mama, popo pesti *(peste* — plague), koma (coma), kurbura *(courbature* — ache), and kana (cane). Still other words are variations on Greek and, more often, Latin words with endings similar to those of Latin declensions — *i, a, um,* and *us.* Finally, it seems highly likely that Artaud drew certain words from historical incantations. He was acquainted with the book *La magie assyrienne: Etude suivi de textes magiques* (Paris, 1902), which contains numerous ancient Assyrian incantations that the author, Charles Fossey, had translated into French. Many of the magic syllables found in these incantations crop up in Artaud's poetry. Some of them denote parts of the body and were used in rituals designed to cure sickness and disease: ka (mouth), eme (tongue), ma (womb). Still others refer to the process of exorcism itself: enim-enim-ma (exorcism), ta-mat (be exorcised), tu-tu (incantation). (Greene, p. 214)

"scabrazage": Based on Artaud's coined "escharrasage," which appears to be based on "escharre" (scab), "raser" (to raze), with the suffix "-age."

"li tigation": Based on "litige" (litigation). By separating "li" from "tige," Artaud suggests "la tige" (the stem). "tige" in slang can mean "penis," and given the fact that "penis" appears as such in the preceding paragraph, chances are it evoked the sexually-oriented pun.

335

Artaud the Mômo

OC XII, 1974, pp. 10-63. The poems, or texts, that make up the complete work were written between July and September, 1946. It is the first major work that Artaud started and completed after his release from Rodez, and on this level, it may be thought of as a bristling declaration that he is back. The work was originally published as a book by Bordas, in January, 1948, with eight drawings by Artaud. As in the case of many texts created after leaving Rodez, *Artaud the Mômo* was begun in notebooks (the "dossier" of worksheets takes up 124 pages in *OC* XII), then dictated to an assistant, after which it was corrected in typescript and in several sets of proofs. *Artaud the Mômo* is probably Artaud's most honed and polished work.

"Mômo" is Marseilles slang for simpleton, or village idiot, and as we understand it, "Artaud the Mômo" is the phoenix-like figure which rose from the ashes of the death of "the old Artaud" probably in electroshock in Rodez in 1943 or 1944. "The Return of Artaud, the Mômo" might be understood as the return of Artaud, now as a Mômo, to the world of imagination, as well as to literary life in Paris.

One must also take into consideration this word's relation to the Greek god of mockery and raillery, Momus, said by Hesiod to be the son of Sleep and Night, the nocturnal voice of Hermes, bearing in his hand a crotalum (in contrast to a caduceus). Because of the rich associations of Mômo/Momus, we have decided not to translate the word. As in the case of the word "negritude" in the work of Aimé Césaire, Artaud seems to have possessed the word and, in poetry, made it his own.

"It's the penetral. . . anayor": This quatrain contains a complex web of sound and association, some of which is untranslatable. Soundwise, there is the play on "toile," "pentrale," "poile," "voile," and "anale," as well as on "ou" which occurs four times. "Poil" (fur or hair) is normally masculine; here Artaud has feminized it, by adding an "e," so that it matches "toile" and "voile." It happens that "poile" does exist, as an archaic form of "poêle" (a toga, mantle, cloak, or pall). Since "poêle" is masculine, we should probably rule it out as the meaning of the (now) feminine "la poile." However, it is very tempting to accept the archaic and masculine "poile" as Artaud's intention, since as a "pall" it metaphorically rhymes with the web ("toile d'araignée") and, in its masculine form, "voile" as veil (in contrast to the feminine meaning, sail). It is tempting to go for web, pall, and veil, which strongly evoke "the veil of Isis," or feminine mystery, which Artaud seems to be evoking in this quatrain (to some extent contradicted by the last line). However, there is no reason to assume that the usually quite precise Artaud became gender careless in this quatrain, so while we make a few adjustments to coax as much play out of the quatrain as possible, we respect the feminine pronouns.

"onor" Appears to be old French for "honor." There is a slight possibility that Artaud had Onuris, a god from Upper Egypt in mind. "la plaque anale" (anal plate) is possibly explained by the following definition of a chastity belt (from *The Book of Lists,* Bantam, 1980): "a leather-covered iron hoop to which were attached a frontal plate with a saw-toothed slit and an anal plate, which had a small opening." While the "ana" of "anavou" picks up the "ana" in "anale," we also hear "à vous" in "avou" and, given our attempt to parallel the French "ou" sounds with "or" sounds in English, render it as "yor" (a playful contraction of "your").

"old bag": A much-pondered solution for "carne," which the *Dictionnaire érotique* (Payot, 1993) defines as "femme, au sens de 'vieux cheval'; péjoratif traditionnel de la femme." The word, however, does not appear to be that simple, with Harraps defining it as: 1. (a) tough meat; (b) old horse; screw. 2. (a) bad-tempered person; (of man) can-tankerous brute; (of woman) bitch; (b) wastrel, bad egg; (of woman) slut." The word's appearance in the poem, as "une carne," seems to register a kind of woman, rather than meat. However, in one of the early drafts for this section (*OC* XII, p. 116), Artaud replaces "viande" (meat) with "carne" in the line: "cette carne entre deux genoux," indi-cating that "carne" may be a substitute, in the section, for "viande." It appears to be impossible to translate "carne" in a single word as low-quality or tough meat. To try to do so is to be forced into such words as "gristle" or "mutton," for example, which signal meaning associations that are irrelevant. While "old bag" probably compromises to some extent the denotative density of "carne," it plays off "hole" and "palm" in fasci-nating ways.

"alienage": A coined cognate for "alienage," which appears to have been coined, in French, by Artaud.

"copulize": Based on "copule," coined by Artaud apparently off "copulation" (copula-tion).

"pussy-toady": "chatte-mite" appears to be a cognate for the English "catamite" but this is not so. A "chattemite" is a sanctimonious person, a toady. By hyphenating "chatte-mite," Artaud emphasizes "chatte" (slang for "pussy").

"frockets": Based on *"froche,"* which appears to have been invented by Artaud. It plays off "poche" (pocket) in the line above, as well as off "toucher" (to touch) and "frôler" (to rub or brush).

"clogation": Based on "colmatations," which appears to be an Artaud variation on "colmatage" (plugging, clogging).

"tench": Archaic slang for "vagina." It is used here to match "moniche" (archaic thieves' slang for the same). "Moniche" rhymes with "boniche" in the same passage; thus our choice of "tench" to rhyme with "wench."

"mamtram": Probably coined off "mantra," a sacred Sanskrit text or a Tantric spell. It is impossible to know if this is a mishearing on Artaud's part, or his play, possibly, on "mama" and "trame" (woof, plot). Artaud's work is furrowed with mommy plots.

"perisprit": A rare synonym for the fluid envelope, or astral body, that in certain occult lore is believed to exist between the body and the spirit. Artaud must have spotted "père" (father) and "esprit" (spirit) in the word.

"when he was himself. . . and THAT": Literally, this passage might have been translated as "when he was himself, what, law, me, king, you, damnit and THAT." Since all these words rhyme in French, we have given priority to the sound here.

"swallowing": "déglutinant" seems to be based on "déglutiner" (and not on "déglutir," to swallow), a rare word that refers to removing bird lime (the "glu") from a bird's feathers, as an aspect of hunting. Since this word is juxtaposed with "mastiquant" (chewing), we translate it as "swallowing." The alternative would simply look bizarre, and obscure the obvious connection between swallowing and chewing.

INDIAN CULTURE

OC XII, pp. 69-74. Originally published with *Here Lies* as a single book, by K editeur, in 1948, the two poems were both written on a single day, November 25, 1946. Both began in notebooks, and were subsequently dictated to Artaud's assistant, after which the poems were typed and corrected.

"the pusseying father": "mimire" appears to be a coined, compound word, based on "mimi" (pussycat, and by extension the sexual "pussy"), and "mirer" (to take aim at, or to look closely at, to eye).

"the hollow mamuffin": "mamiche" also appears to be coined and compound, based on "mama" and "miche" (a round loaf of bread; in the plural, in the proper context, it can refer to buttocks). In the cases of "mimire" and "mimiche" we have sought to create compound words in English in which, as in the French, the end of one word is the beginning of the next.

"daddy-mommy": Probably the mundane "primal scene" as a caricature of the Father-Mother ("père-mère") conjunction, in Tibetan Buddhism known as Yab-Yum, transcendentally one of the manifestations of the Buddha. In the opening lines of the poem that follows *Indian Culture*, Artaud will suggest that the transcendental father-mother is merely a projection of daddy-mommy primal scene, which is embedded in his body. As the race of Amalakites are said to spring directly from the earth, and as the Tarahumaras "eat Peyote straight from the soil/while it is being born," so does Artaud, a parental system unto himself, bear his daughters directly from his own heart while he watches them being destroyed by forces committed to a sexual leveling of life.

"tusk hole": "boutis" is a rare word referring to the holes in fields made by boars rooting with their tusks.

HERE LIES

OC XII, pp. 75-100. Like the opening section of *Artaud the Mômo,* the opening section of *Here Lies* is heavily rhymed. Such rhyming, which falls in obsessive clusters rather than in any formal or conventional pattern, introduces a nursery-rhyme-like element into a visionary argument, giving a unique "veer" to the writing. We have refrained from attempting to match this rhyming because to do so plays havoc with the meaning.

"pantabazooms": Artaud's *"falzourchte"* appears to be coined and augmented off "falzar," argot for trousers. The coined suffix recalls sounds that appeared in the chant ending "The Return of Artaud, the Mômo." Our word plays with pantaloons, linking it to a raffish word for big female breasts.

"the viper (father life)": Artaud plays on "vipère" (viper) and, suggested by the "vie mère" (mother life) above it, "vie père" (father life).

"scrubby grope slope/croupswarmed": "parpougnête" appears to be coined off "far-fouiller," which conventionally means to rummage about, and erotically means to grope or fuck. The suffix is ironic, tender, and pejorative. "engruper" is also coined, and appears to be formed from such words as "agripper" (to clutch, seize), "agrouper" (to group) and "croup" (rump, croup, crupper etc.). Our thanks to Jean-Pierre Auxeméry and Daniel Delas for useful input here.

"And that is how. . . all the sooners": For a brief but insightful commentary on this section, see Julia Kristeva's "l'Engendrement de la formule," *Tel quel* #38, 1969, pp. 58-59.

"nolarking. . . titrating you": The passage is packed with word particles. We built our version off "alouette" (lark) which led us to "malarkey." We chose to keep the sound play of *"tirant"* *"titrant,"* forcing us to mistranslate *"tirant"* (shooting, or fucking).

"stud-in-law": Based on Artaud's "gendron," which appears to be coined off "gendre" (son-in-law), to which an augmentative suffix has been added.

"All true language. . . (bloodied)": As a feminine noun, "claque" can refer to a slap, a claque (paid clappers), or kicking the bucket. A "claquedent" (in the text the hyphen is Artaud's) is a miserable wretch, a brothel, or a clapperdudgeon (a beggar born). "claque" as a masculine noun is an opera hat, or a brothel. By adding "bordel" to the line, Artaud signals that he prefers the cathouse meaning of the word here, so we play with "clap-trap," conventionally a trick to gain applause or insincere sentiment, but in our version of Artaud heaven it is that trap in which one gets the clap.

FROM INTERJECTIONS

OC XIV**, 1978, pp. 43-44, 46-47, 48-50, 52-54, 55, 59-60, 62, 63-64, 68-69, 137-145, 149. These fourteen dictations are from *Suppôts et suppliciations* (the title of which inspired the title of this book). This is the last book-length work that Artaud himself edited; it is made up of ten essays, thirty-five letters, and seventy-three dictations. He described it in the following way:

type of book absolutely impossible to read,
that no one has ever read from end to end,
not even its author,
because it does not exist
but is the fruit of a consortium of incubi and succubi nailed, stabbed,
    planted everywhere,
pullulating, in the body of Man,
turned over and over like a turkey on the grill. (*OC* XIV**, p. 234)

As for the dictations: while in the Ivry clinic, Artaud signed a contract for the book which would become *Suppôts*. The would-be publisher, Louis Broder, hired a young secretary to visit Artaud every morning and to take down by hand material that he would dictate to her. These dictations were then, as usual, typed up and corrected/revised by Artaud.

The dictation period ran from November 1946 to February 1947, and actually appears to include a modest portion of Artaud's proclamations from this period. He would break into dictation at any time — while in bed, at a café table, or with friends — only to suddenly interrupt himself and become absorbed in a long silence. Luciane Abiet would arrive early in the morning at Artaud's room, often when Artaud, still sleepy, would be sitting up in bed, his café au lait cooling on the bedside table. Abiet's difficulties in getting down exactly what Artaud said were compounded by the fact that he was missing all his teeth and often fighting hesitations brought about by chloral hydrate or other drugs.

THE HUMAN FACE

L'Ephémère #13, 1970, pp. 45-48. This brief essay was the preface to an exposition of Artaud's drawings held at the Galerie Pierre Loeb, from the 4th to the 20th of July, 1947. "The Human Face" compliments Artaud's longer essay on van Gogh (ably translated by Helen Weaver). Stephen Barber writes: "In particular, [Artaud's] drawings of the human face — the only remaining authentic element of the anatomy for Artaud — endeavor to obliterate the body's weaknesses and to return it to a vivid manifestation of turbulent movement and experience. The facial features of his drawings — hard bones and concentrated eyes — challenge and reformulate the visual world through the dynamism of their individual creativity." (Barber, p. 3)

NOTES

To Have Done With The Judgement of God
The Theater of Cruelty
Open Letter to the Reverend Father Laval

OC XIII, 1974, pp 67-118, 142-145. I have commented on the circumstances of Artaud's radio work in the Introduction. "The Theater of Cruelty" which is part of *To Have Done With* should not be confused with the earlier essay with the same title; the work here was written as part of *To Have Done With* but not recorded with the five-section work because of time limitations. It is unequaled as a brief summation of Artaud's final thoughts on human anatomy and destiny.

After the broadcast was banned, Pouey assembled a literary jury to hear the recording, which they unanimously supported. Among them, curiously enough, was a Father Laval who besides voting enthusiastically for the broadcast attempted to meet Artaud soon after. Artaud did not appreciate the publicity that a priest's intervention brought, and to end the matter sent Laval an Open Letter.

Of the letters written by Artaud concerning the interdiction affair, twelve were published by Gallimard in *OC* XIII, of which Helen Weaver translated seven, omitting the letter to Laval. We have selected this particular one because it is the only letter which refers to and elucidates important themes that recur in *To Have Done With,* and which also stands as an independent text in its own right.